Create Your Family Quilt

Using State Blocks and Symbols

Barbara Brackman

The Electric Quilt Company

Brackman, Barbara
Create Your Family Quilt
Using State Blocks and Symbols /
Barbara Brackman
p.   cm.
ISBN 1-893824-10-1 (pbk.)

Published by The Electric Quilt Company
419 Gould Street, Suite 2
Bowling Green, OH 43402
www.electricquilt.com

Printed in China
10 9 8 7 6 5 4 3 2 1

Book
Executive Editor: Dean Neumann
Editor: Penny McMorris
Copy Editor: Diane McEwen-Martin
Book Design: Rayanne Turek
Cover Design: Jill Badenhop
Photography: Mark Packo
Photographic Assistant: Mark Kurczewski

Software
Development: Dean Neumann
        Ann Rutter
Graphics: Rachel Reulbach
        Monica Vay
Block Colorings: Margaret Okuley

In memory of Louise Owens Townsend

As always, I have relied on my circle of friends for help.
Patti Butcher, Shauna Christensen, Susannah Christenson,
Pam Mayfield, bobbi-frances mcdonald, Jean Stanclift
and Sharon Vesecky designed and made quilts.
And thanks to Cuesta Benberry, Joyce Gross and Merikay Waldvogel
who have generously let me use their pattern collections
to assemble information on the state designs.

An American family about 1910.

Table of Contents

A California sewing group.

About the Author

Barbara Brackman

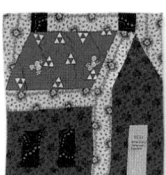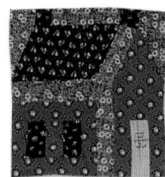

Barbara Brackman has lived in six states and visited 48. That's the kind of information she likes to keep track of. She views information as a collectible, and much of her life has delighted in making lists and files of all sorts of things. This book on state patterns grew out of a fascination with quilt patterns and ways to index them. In the 1970s she began writing articles for *Quilter's Newsletter Magazine*, giving readers collections of patterns named for places, holidays, occupations, pets and people.

Barbara was born in New York City, grew up in Ohio and Kansas and has lived in Lawrence, Kansas since she went to college there in the early '60s. Periodically she moves to a big city for an urban adventure, but Lawrence always draws her back.

Besides quilt patterns, she collects antique fabrics and clothing, dishes, information on environmental folk art, women's diaries, Kansas trivia, women during the Civil War, cowboy costumes and photographs of dogs. Each of these collections eventually winds up in a museum exhibition or book.

Right now she is working on a history of territorial Kansas, a history of the dog (with her sister), and a book on fabrics in antique quilts. She is the president of a local charity, which runs a thrift store, has been doing the pattern of the month for her guild, and is supervising the replacement of the front porch on her Victorian house. She lives with a small black dog.

*Home Arts magazine mapped American craft
in this 1938 cover by Mary Sherwood Wright-Jones.*

Introduction

Each family draws its identity from many sources—religious and ethnic backgrounds, stories and customs, jokes and tragedies. A sense of place is also important to family history. This book gives you a repertoire of state quilt block patterns to incorporate your, or your whole family's, sense of place into family quilts. And it gives you a sense of those quilt blocks' own history in the quilting tradition.

*P*lace is important. Americans always want to know where you're from. What a gift to be able to say Slippery Rock, Pennsylvania, or Pretty Prairie, Kansas! America's place names are a poetry we never tire of hearing. Place names tell us about our past. Mississippi and New Paltz, Oconomowoc and LaJolla, Springfield and Louisville echo many cultures. Carolina, New York and Georgia tell us of our days as a British colony; Arkansas, Tennessee and Alaska of the time when the Native Tribes named the land. Place names tell us what we value – heroes such as Washington and Lincoln and things brand new as in New Mexico and New Hampshire, dramatic landscapes like Colorado, Montana and Rocky Mount and the honest plainness of Midland and Normal.

We also hear a poetry in the names of our quilt patterns – **Richmond Beauty**, **Missouri Puzzle**, **Kansas Troubles**, **Carolina Lily**. This book and CD program combine American place names with American quilt design, giving you patterns named for the fifty states plus Canada's provinces and territories. Names for the traditional pieced designs come from quilt historians, pattern indexes and newspaper columns of the past. It also features new appliqué designs for the birds, flowers and trees assigned to each state, to be used for the quilt border.

Most state quilt blocks were named by magazines in the twentieth century. We have little evidence that mid-nineteenth century quilters called their quilts by such poetic descriptions; they left no records.

Most of the material about the traditional state patterns first appeared in *Quilter's Newsletter Magazine*. The whole idea of articles on state patterns originated with an article about Arkansas pieced patterns in 1978, and ended with Minnesota eighteen years later. Louise O. Townsend, to whom this book is dedicated, was managing editor at *Quilter's Newsletter Magazine* much of that time. We had fun planning the sequence, timing the articles to bicentennials, sesquicentennials and special events. Louise wrote the article about Maryland, her home state.

Pattern designers used different pen names in different periodicals. The "Virginia Star" is from the McKim Studios, but appeared in the Jane Friendly column in the San Francisco Chronicle.

Before I had *BlockBase* (the CD-ROM version of my book, the *Encyclopedia of Pieced Quilt Patterns*), my method of researching state quilt blocks was to go to the library to make a list of a state's attributes and history, then read through the alphabetic index in the back of my *Encyclopedia* until a pattern name caught my eye. I'd find names as obvious as **Journey to California** and **Arkansas Traveler** and as far-fetched as **Polka Dot** for Wisconsin or **Letha's Electric Fan** for Arizona. I'd draw sketches of each design and send them to Louise who'd ask the staff artists to paste fabric mock-ups of the blocks and design a sampler for each state.

Back then, *Quilter's Newsletter Magazine's* publisher, Bonnie Leman, Louise and I discussed publishing a book of all the state patterns. But when we calculated how many designs we'd found over nearly two decades, we realized we had more than 500 patterns, far too much material for a paper-based book. When Penny McMorris and Dean Neumann, at The Electric Quilt Company, showed me the BlockBase CD-ROM, I knew the time had come to do a book/computer combination with hundreds of digital patterns in infinite sizes. With this book, and the over 700 blocks on the accompanying CD, you can design a unique quilt to symbolize your own family's story and sense of place.

State Patterns in Quilt History

My articles in *Quilter's Newsletter Magazine* weren't the first on state quilt block patterns. In 1907, Mary E. Bradford, the editor of the Useful and Fancywork page for *Hearth and Home* magazine, asked readers to mail in piecework cloth blocks named for the various states. Of the entries, she would pick one to represent that state, and publish a black and white photo or pattern sketch. For a nickel, readers could buy a pattern diagram. The forty-eight states required five years of issues. Bradford then asked for blocks named for U. S. Possessions such as Guam and Hawaii. A third series of quilt blocks named for state capitals ran until 1916.

Hearth and Home's readers traded quilt and crochet patterns in the column and calico blocks and signatures through the mail.

Hearth and Home's state pattern collection reflected the interest in travel at a time when automobiles and postcards were new ideas. Americans were crazy about souvenirs. Vacationers displayed stones from the deserts and mountains in their backyard rock gardens, and pasted Brownie camera photos into travel albums. Even stay-at-homes could collect postcards, a hobby encouraged by *Hearth and Home's* sister magazine *Comfort,* which matched pen pals. The postcard of New Haven on page 46 was sent to Maude Shelby in Oklahoma City by an impatient stranger. "I saw your name in Comfort. Would be pleased to exchange cards with you. Should like views of Okla. very much. Do write soon it takes to [sic] long."

Readers could also exchange quilt blocks with pen pals found in the Fancywork columns, making one believe that somewhere there are sampler quilts made up of *Hearth and Home* blocks – or, as is more likely, stacks of blocks still waiting to be made up into sampler quilts.

11

About the same time that *Hearth and Home's* pattern series was running, state legislatures were designating "official" state flowers, choosing a typical native to represent their image. States also chose official birds and then trees, actions designed to create an awareness of our natural treasures and an appreciation for the commonplace. While federal and state governments set aside national parks and forests, they also promoted conservation by outlawing the killing of song birds, and giving children a personal connection to wildlife through the state symbol program.

Do You Know Your State Flowers?

From the Omaha World-Herald.

By the 1930s, a fashion for outline-embroidered quilt patterns combined with the state symbol movement in several series of quilt blocks to be sewn with colored cotton floss. Ruby McKim's *State Flower* series may be the first of these now classic designs. McKim's pattern series was syndicated to various newspapers, appearing in the *Omaha World-Herald* in September, 1931. McKim indicated that her embroidery patterns could also be appliquéd, but most who made up the state symbol patterns embroidered them. And some quiltmakers in the latter twentieth century used felt tip fabric markers to copy state bird and flower patterns on fabric in a technique called Liquid Embroidery. Although the embroidered state patterns have been popular with the average quiltmaker who is grateful for the simplicity of a stamped kit, they never captured the attention of the more sophisticated quilter who wants to exercise creativity in technique, design and fabric choice. I've found no state bird, flower or tree series for piecing or appliqué.

Ruby Short McKim's State Flowers Quilt in embroidery.

Ruby Short McKim designed a second state pattern series. Her pieced *Patchwork Parade of States* was syndicated to newspapers in the early 1930s. Soon after, *Workbasket* magazine designed a pieced *All-State Quilt*. I've never seen an actual quilt made up in either of these designs, which consisted of traditional blocks assigned symbolically – for example, Yankee Puzzle for Connecticut or a Pine Tree for Maine. It's evident that the embroidered pattern series were far more popular with needleworkers.

Pattern designers sometimes recorded traditional names, but often changed them to appeal to the customer. H. H. Ver Mehnen's Omaha pattern company was one of several that called the traditional "Rocky Mountain" "New York Beauty".

Both McKim and *Workbasket* were located in Kansas City, Missouri, an indication of how important that area was to quilt pattern history in the mid-twentieth century and the reason so many patterns are named for Missouri – the state with the most pieced blocks. Sources like the Ladies Art Company in St. Louis and the *Kansas City Star* newspaper published numerous patterns named for their home state over the years. By comparison, Maryland and Delaware, important to nineteenth-century quiltmaking but home to no commercial pattern companies, can claim few pattern names.

The location of pattern studios is not the only reason why one state has more patterns than another. Both California and Texas boast many designs, yet neither has been home to significant pattern sources. Texas and California, like Kansas, are more than mere places. In the nineteenth century, they were crusades, as Robert Smith Bader has noted in his study of the Kansas image, *Hayseeds, Moralizers and Methodists* (University Press of Kansas, 1988). The press painted vivid pictures of California and its gold, Texas and its Alamo, and "Bleeding" Kansas with its Civil War troubles – images with broad appeal to Americans fascinated with the west. "Rocky Road to Kansas" and "Texas Tears" reflect a national preoccupation with particular regions. So the quilter who wants to remember the family home in Topeka or Tyler has more designs to choose from than the quilter from Tupelo or Trenton.

Ruth Finley, in her book Old Patchwork Quilts And The Women Who Made Them, told many stories of quilt pattern names.

During the 1970s and '80s, a few quilt designers published booklets on their particular state. Jean Mitchell's *Quilt Kansas!* was typical, in that she included traditional patterns and a few of her own design. These booklets are now mostly out-of-print and hard-to-find. I have a stack of eleven such pattern booklets on my desk, and I've included the reference under each state if I know of a late-twentieth century booklet. The best place to start looking for them is your quilt guild and local library.

How to Use the CD

Follow the installation instructions found on the inside back cover to install the Magic Book software. The Magic Book software lets you design your own family quilt as well as print patterns for any of the blocks shown in this book. To help you get started, we will guide you, step-by-step, through the designing of a quilt. This lesson, which takes about 20 minutes to complete, is intended to give you a quick overview of how to use the software so that you can begin designing right away. We strongly suggest that you consult the online help for complete instructions on all the features of the Magic Book software.

1. Double-click on the **Create a Family Quilt** icon found on the Desktop (or in the **Electric Quilt** group) to start.

2. Position the mouse cursor over the words **Begin Designing Your Quilt** and click.  *Begin Designing Your Quilt*

3. For your first family quilt, imagine you want to make a small wallhanging for your parents' 50ᵗʰ wedding anniversary. The first step is to choose a border design. Click the first border choice – the **top-left quilt**. You want a simple border, so you don't have too much appliqueing to do.

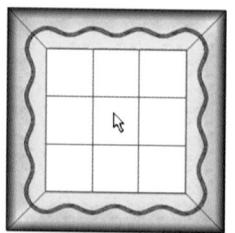

4. Next you'll choose the size for your quilt. Click the **Crib Size** quilt, 44 x 44 inches. You want a small quilt, to fit over your father's favorite chair. Notice that this 4-block quilt can be used for *Crib Size* *44 x 44 inches* wallhangings as well as crib quilts. This screen gives you a summary of your quilt layout including the number of blocks and the overall size. Now you're ready to select the pieced blocks for the center of your quilt and the appliqué motifs for the border. The number of blocks and motifs you choose is totally up to you. Barbara Brackman offers some suggestions found in the chart on page 24.

5. Position the mouse cursor over the words **I'm ready to select blocks** and click. You'll see a map appear.

I'm ready to select blocks

6. Click **West**. Your parents live in California. So you want to get a California block for your quilt's center. You'll see an enlarged view of the states included in the region.

7. Click **California**. The blocks and motifs for California will appear. Notice the Block Palette found on the lower-left corner of the screen. This is where you will put the blocks you want to use in your quilt. As you position the mouse cursor over a block or motif a tooltip will appear showing the name of the block. Rest the cursor over each pieced block in the top row. Look for the purple block, (4ᵗʰ from left) one of several blocks called *Rocky Road to California*. This block could remind your parents of how they drove to California for their honeymoon in 1951 and loved the state so much they settled there.

8. To select this block, position the mouse cursor over it. Press and hold down the left mouse button as you drag the block to the Block Palette at the bottom-left of the screen. You'll see the block move as you drag. Position the block directly over the Block Palette and release the left mouse button. You'll see the block shrink into the palette. Notice the block's original position is now faded indicating that the block has been moved to the palette. (If the block does not appear faded, then you did not select it. Try dragging the block again making sure that it is positioned directly over the Block Palette before you drop it.)

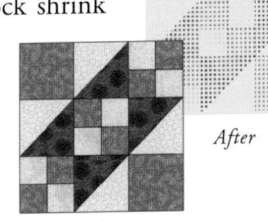

After

Before

9. Position the mouse cursor over the words, **Go to another state** and click. You'll be back to the map.

Go to another state

10. For this sample lesson, you are from New Jersey. You'll go there to select a motif for the border to represent you. Click the **Atlantic** region.

11. Click on **New Jersey**.

12. The motifs for each state are always at the top of the screen. Violets are your mother's favorite flower. Drag the *Violet* motif to the Block Palette and drop it. The violet motif will appear faded.

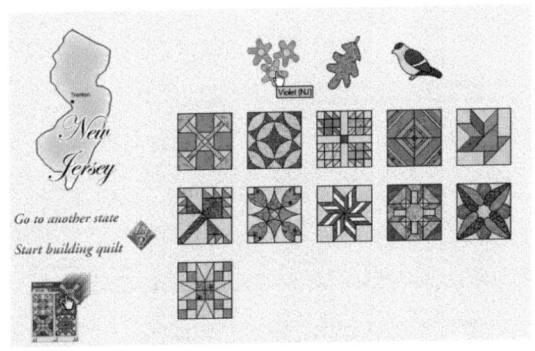

15

13. Click on **Go to another state**. You'll be back to the map. You want to select other motifs to represent your brothers and sisters. Here are your imaginary brothers and sisters and the states they live in. Use the map to go to each state and put the suggested motif into the Block Palette.

> Bill – Southeast – Florida – Mockingbird. (Bill's got a sharp wit.)
> Barb – Northwest – Idaho – Mountain Bluebird. (Barb owns the Bluebird Café.)
> Beth – Southwest – Kansas – Sunflower. (Beth is always happy.)
> Bob – Great Lakes – Wisconsin – Sugar Maple. (Bob is a carpenter.)
> Ben – Northwest – Wyoming – Indian Paintbrush. (Ben's an artist.)
> Bonnie – Northwest – Oregon – Grape. (Bonnie works at a winery.)
> Bruce – Southwest – Oklahoma – Redbud. (Bruce's nickname is "Red.")

14. When you are done collecting blocks and motifs from the different states, click on **Start building quilt**. (These words *Start building quilt* appear on all the state screens.)

15. Now you will see the screen where you will do all of the designing of your quilt. Notice the tools along the top of the screen. Notice the Block Palette along the right. It contains all the blocks and motifs you just selected. (To see the motifs, click on the **Motif** tab.) Notice the tabs **Pieced Layer** and **Applique Layer** along the lower-left of the screen. The quilt and border you selected at the beginning will be displayed. The quilt has some simple generic leaves already placed on the vine to get you started. The white circles represent *place-holders* for more appliqué motifs. You will be able to place motifs in the white circles and replace any of the leaves as well as delete them.

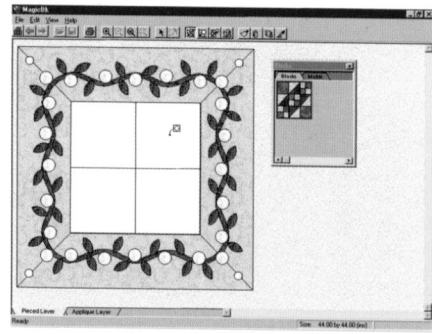

16. The first step you'll do is to set the pieced *Rocky Road to California* block into the center of the quilt. To set blocks be sure the **Set Block tool** is selected by clicking on it. Again you can position the mouse cursor over the tool for the name to appear.

17. Click the **Pieced Layer** tab beneath your quilt.

18. Click on the *Rocky Road to California* block in the Block Palette. The block is framed in blue, showing it is the selected block.

19. Point to an empty block space in the center of your quilt and click. The block will pop into your quilt. Click in all four spaces to set the block in all the center spaces.

20. Now you'll set some appliqué motifs on the border. You will continue to use the **Set Block tool** 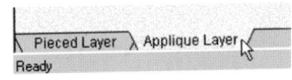 so you don't need to change tools, but you need to change layers. Click the **Applique Layer** tab beneath your quilt.

21. Click on the Motifs tab in the Block Palette to see the motifs. The motifs you selected earlier are here. Drag the scrollbar along the bottom of the palette to see all the motifs. You'll notice a blue frame that indicates the selected motif. Find the *Sunflower* and click on it so the blue frame surrounds it.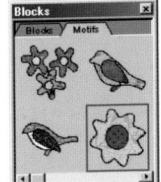

22. Position the cursor over the center of a white circle on your quilt border and click to set the *Sunflower* motif in that spot. Continue to click on other white circles to set the *Sunflower* in other spots.

23. Find the *Redbud* leaf motif in the Block Palette and click on it to select it.

24. Now click on one of the generic leaves in the quilt. It will be replaced with the *Redbud* leaf. Continue to replace several generic leaves with the *Redbud* leaf. If you like, try to set motifs until your quilt looks roughly like the one illustrated at the right. All of your brothers and sisters need to be represented so be sure to set at least one of each motif.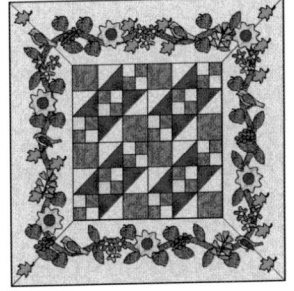

25. 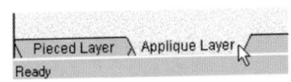 Now you'll go back and work on the center of the quilt. Remember that it is the pieced layer so you'll need to change layers. Click on the **Pieced Layer** tab beneath your quilt.

26. Let's try the **Rotate tool**. Click on the **Rotate tool**  to select it. The Block Palette will close, and your mouse cursor will change to a ⟲. Click on the blocks in the center until you have them rotated as illustrated here.

27. Many of the tools will work with the **Ctrl** and **Alt** keys on your keyboard. Just for fun, try holding down the **Ctrl** key while you click with the Rotate tool. All the blocks on that layer will rotate at once. Do the same with the **Alt** key. It will rotate alternating blocks at once. (Note: For some blocks you will not notice rotation because they are the same on all sides.)

28. Now you'll go back and work on the appliqué border of the quilt. Click on the **Applique Layer** tab beneath your quilt.

29. Since the **Rotate tool** is still selected, if you'd like to rotate any of the motifs click directly on the motif to rotate it.

30. You can also flip blocks and motifs. Click on the **Flip tool** [icon] to select it.

31. Now click on any motif to flip it. Try it on one of the birds because you can easily see the difference. Some of the flowers – the *Sunflower* for example – won't show much of a change when using the **Rotate tool** or the **Flip tool**. If your motif ends up underneath another motif, don't worry. You'll learn how to move motifs using the **Adjust tool**.

32. Since the anniversary is quickly approaching, you don't have much time for appliquéing. To simplify the border, you want to delete some of the motifs and rearrange the ones that are left. To do this, you'll need to use the **Adjust tool**.

33. Click on the **Adjust tool** [icon] to select it.

34. Click on a motif that you want to delete. You'll know it is selected by the frame that appears around it.

35. Press the **Delete** key on your keyboard. The motif will be gone. Continue to delete as many motifs as you like. (Note: If you accidentally delete the wrong motif, choose **Undo** from the **Edit** menu (or press **Ctrl+Z**) to undo your most recent action.)

36. To change a motif's position on the border, click on the motif you want to move. Press and hold the left mouse button and drag the motif to the new position. Release the mouse to drop the motif in the new location. Click somewhere outside of the quilt to deselect the motif. Continue to delete and rearrange the border until you are satisfied.

37. All of the blocks come pre-colored with fabric for you. If you'd like to change the fabrics you can. We'll pretend you're very happy with your border including the way it is colored. Now you'd like to recolor the center of the quilt with the fabrics used in the border. You'll use the **Eyedropper tool** [icon] first so click on it to select it. The Fabric Palette will appear.

38. You really like the golden color used on the petals of the *Sunflower* motif. You've scrolled through the fabrics in the palette, and you're not sure which one it is. The **Eyedropper** will help you find it. Be sure you're still on the **Applique Layer** and then click on the *Sunflower* petal. The fabric will be selected for you. Now you're ready to paint on the bottom layer.

39. [icon: Pieced Layer / Applique Layer tabs] Click on the **Pieced Layer** tab.

40. Click on the **Spraycan tool**. [icon]

41. Click on one of the bright yellow patches in the center of the quilt. Notice that all the yellow patches in that block are recolored at the same time with the golden color. The

Spraycan tool recolors all matching patches in one block.

42. Press and hold the **Ctrl** key, and click on another bright yellow patch in another block. The rest of your bright yellow patches will be recolored with the golden color.

43. Click on the **Paintbrush tool.** This tool will color patches one at a time.

44. Scroll to the very last fabric in the palette to select it.

45. Click on the border. One side of the border will recolor. Click on the other three sides of the border. It's important to remember that this large mitered border is part of the pieced layer. To recolor the rest of the elements on the border – the vine, leaves and other motifs – you need to change to the **Applique layer.**

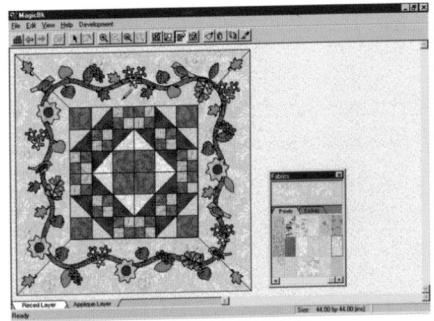

46. Continue to color until you are satisfied with your quilt. If you would like to save this quilt permanently as a file on your computer's hard drive, choose **Save** from the **File** menu and type in a name for your quilt. A good name for this quilt would be **My First Family Quilt**. It's always a good idea to save your quilt. You probably won't want to print all of the patterns for making the quilt at the same time. Since you can save your design, you can print the patterns as you are ready to use them.

47. You would like to print Rotary Cutting instructions for the *Rocky Road to California* block and templates for the *Sunflower* motif. There are many different printing options. Be sure to consult the online help (choose **Magic Book Help** from the **Help** menu) for a complete discussion of all the printing options.

48. Click on the **Select tool.** You need to select the block you want to print with this tool. Click on one of the blocks in the center of the quilt.

49. Click on the **Print tool** on the toolbar.

50. Click on **Rotary Cutting...** The Rotary Cutting Instructions dialog box will appear.

51. The block size in the quilt is 12 inches. You'll see the size is set to 12 x 12 for you. If you'd like to print the pattern in a different size, select **Let me set the size**, and type in the size you want for the width and height. You want the instructions for a 12 inch block so don't make any changes in the dialog box.

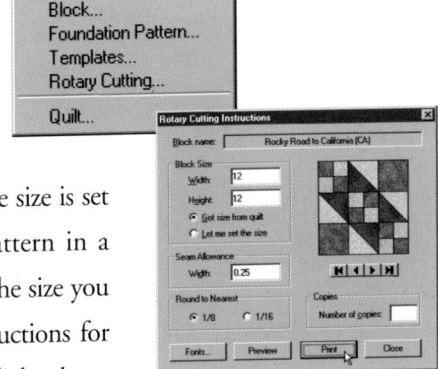

52. Click the **Preview** button.

53. Click **Print**. _Remember that the rotary cutting instructions are for **1 block**. You'll be making **4 blocks** for the center of your quilt._

54. Click the **Applique Layer** tab beneath your quilt.

55. You're still using the **Select tool** so simply click on the _Sunflower_ motif.

56. Click on the **Print tool** on the toolbar.

57. Click on **Templates…** The Print Template dialog box will appear.

58. All of the motifs that are set into the big circles are 4.75 inches by 4.75 inches. The motifs set in the small circles (which includes the replacements for the generic leaves) are 3 inches by 3 inches. Once again, if you'd like to print the template in a different size, select **Let me set the size**, and type in the size you want for the width and height.

59. Click **Print**. Another way to print applique templates is to choose **Print Block…** and select the printing style **Outline drawing of block**. This will show you the overlapping of the applique patches.

60. You'd like to make one last printout before you're done. Since you own a color printer, you'd like a color printout of your quilt design. Click anywhere outside of the quilt to deselect any block or motif you may have selected.

61. Click on the **Print tool** on the toolbar.

62. Click on **Quilt…** The Print Quilt dialog box will appear.

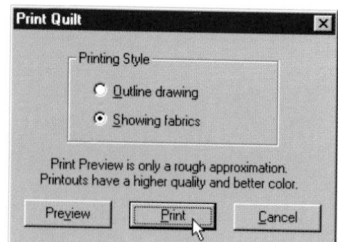

63. Be sure **Showing Fabrics** is selected. Click the **Print** button. The Magic Book software automatically prints the quilt as large as possible on the page.

If you want to print patterns without designing a quilt, you can do that too. You do need to set the block into the quilt layout first and then you can print it. The same is true of the motifs.

 Some screens display a special Help icon. When you click on this icon, you'll see a short video demonstrating various features. Also refer to the online help for additional instructions.

You now have a basic understanding of the steps you'll go through in designing a quilt and printing the patterns. We hope you enjoy creating, designing and making many wonderful family quilts!

How to Make Your Family Quilt

The Family Quilt design consists of a center area of twelve-inch pieced blocks surrounded by a ten-inch border with appliquéd motifs of state birds, flowers and leaves or cones.

The Create Your Family Quilt CD lets you plan quilts on-screen, choosing from four specific layout styles in a variety of sizes, and print patterns perfectly sized for your quilt. But you're not restricted to the CD's layouts, since you can print block and symbol patterns any size you want, and use them to create a quilt without designing it on the computer. Many of the quilts in this book illustrate this free-design style.

Planning Quilt Size

The chart on page 24 will help you plan your quilt whether you're using the CD's automatic layouts or designing your own layout. A king-size quilt, for example, needs a center area 84" square. By adding a ten-inch border on each side, your finished quilt will be 104" square. Your quilt need not be square, but I've done my calculations based on a square. If you recalculate for a rectangular quilt, remember that each side must be divisible by twelve so the border will fit.

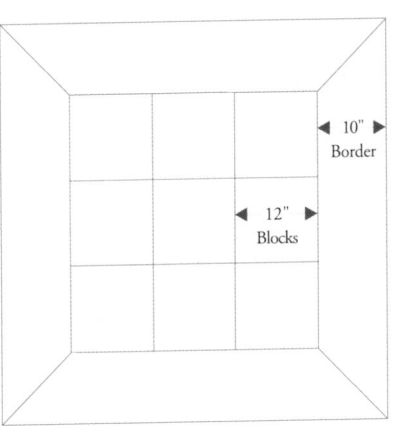

Patterns for Pieced Blocks

The Family Quilt center is made from twelve-inch blocks. Twelve-inch blocks work well, because the quilt borders are designed in twelve-inch increments. Repeat one block, or combine several to make the quilt center, using blocks named for your state, its history and symbols. You may want to pick a single important state. Jean Stanclift, being an enthusiastic Kansas transplant, chose a Kansas Troubles block for her center (fig. 1). You can combine state blocks too, possibly alternating blocks. But your Family Quilt's design will be most dramatic when you repeat one block (the most important state) in the center, then use appliquéd birds, leaves and flowers from various states in the border. For ideas for single patterns for those who've lived in a variety of states, see the Wanderers (page 158).

If you prefer combining blocks of various sizes, you can use any block-size combination that makes a quilt center measurement divisible by twelve. You could piece a framed medallion, as Patti Butcher did for her *Oklahoma* quilt (fig. 2). Or you could piece or appliqué one large block as Pamela Mayfield did for *Hawaii* (fig. 3).

With over 700 patterns on the CD, I can't give piecing instructions. But when choosing patterns for your center, choose easy pieced blocks if you're new to quilting. Straight-lined block patterns, with squares and triangles, are easier to sew than blocks with curves, diamonds or unusual shapes.

Print the block patterns onto sheets of plain printer paper, using your computer printer. If the pattern pieces are too large to fit on one sheet of paper, the CD program will automatically print the rest of the pattern on another sheet. Dotted lines will show you where to overlap the pattern sheets. Match the dotted lines (cut off the overlap) to line up the pattern design. Tape the separate pages together, to form the whole pattern piece. The pattern pieces will include seam allowance, and will make a twelve-inch finished block, unless you specify a different size.

Planning your Border

A ten-inch border is the standard I've used, primarily because a ten-inch border makes the best use of a 44" width of fabric. You'll be able to get four border strips out of the yardage for your background. Cut each strip 10 1/2" wide by the length you'll need for the finished border (add a 1/2" seam allowance to that length). We've calculated yardage based on a mitered border.

fig. 1: Jean Stanclift, Kansas, page 70.

fig. 2: Patti Butcher, Oklahoma, page 116.

fig. 3: Pamela Mayfield, Hawaii, page 58.

fig. 4: Shauna Christensen, Home is Where...♥, page 138.

Patterns for Appliqué Symbols

Choose a state bird, flower and leaf/cone, or think about incorporating symbols from various states. See how Shauna Christensen combined state symbols for her Family Quilt (fig. 4). In the chart on page 24 I suggest the number of appliqué motifs you'll need for a tightly curved border of a particular size. Your best bet is to do your own calculations, however, based on whether your vine is tight or relaxed, and the look you like. If you look at the quilts pictured in the book, you'll note a wide variety of personal choices by each designer.

The vine, birds, flowers and leaves/cones, may be hand or machine-appliquéd. Print the patterns onto plain printer paper. Trace each separate patch in your design onto a different section of freezer paper (available at any grocery store), using a pencil. Be sure to trace a separate pattern for each separate piece in your design. The bird's wings, legs and breast, for example, will usually be separate pieces, each needing their own separate freezer paper pattern.

Cut the designs out of freezer paper, right along your tracing lines. Spread out your fabric, right side up. Put the freezer paper patterns onto the fabric, waxy (shiny) side down. Press the freezer paper patterns to the fabric, using an iron set at the wool setting.

Trace a line around each freezer paper pattern onto the right side of the fabric, using a permanent marker. Cut out the design. For hand-appliqué or invisible machine-appliqué (where raw edges will be turned under), cut 1/8" to 1/4" away from the marked line and freezer paper pattern. For machine-appliqué, sewn over the raw edge, cut your pattern out on the marked line. If you're turning raw edges under, clip inside curves at close intervals, right through the marked line to make turning curves easier.

Bias for Binding and Stems

Fold and press the correct amount of 1/2" bias for your border (see page 29 for information on making bias strips). See the chart for the length you will need. If you want to use stems to connect the flowers and leaves to the vines, you will need more. Stems are optional. If you print the border curve, you'll get a thick curve printout. This is to show you the curve to use with your 1/2" bias strips.

Making Your Own Border Curves

If you study the quilts in this book, you'll notice most of the quilt designers plotted their own border curves and placed their own appliqué motifs. You may like the freedom of creating your own border curves, using some of the pictured quilts as inspiration. This section will describe how to lay out your vine and state bird, flower and leaf symbols free-hand.

Quilt Planning Chart

Quilt Size	Crib	Wall	Throw	Single Bed	Double Bed	King
Inches	44" Square	56" Square	68" Square	80" Square	92" Square	104" Square
Number of 12" Blocks for Center	4	9	16	25	36	49
Center Size Without Borders	24"	36"	48"	60"	72"	84"
Border Yardage for Background	1 1/2	1 3/4	2	2 1/3	2 2/3	3
Yards of Bias Stripping for Vines	5	7	8 3/4	10 1/2	12	14
Suggested Number of Flowers	12	16	20	24	28	32
Suggested Number of Birds	8	12	16	20	24	28
Suggested Number of Leaves	20	28	36	44	52	60

This chart will help you plan your quilt. But since bias stripping yardage and suggested numbers of flowers, birds and leaves may vary according to the quilt you design (my suggestions are for a tight border requiring more appliqué birds, flowers and leaves than a relaxed border), I suggest you use this chart as a guide, but also do your own measurements.

I suggest planning a curve that fits within a twelve-inch border unit length. This fits a curve along the side of a twelve-inch block. You can either have one relaxed curve about twelve inches long, or two tighter curves, each six inches long. The relaxed curve takes fewer appliqué designs, less bias yardage and less time to appliqué. The tighter curve has room for more birds, flowers and leaves. In either case, your border vine should fit an area no wider than nine inches within the ten-inch wide border.

Your border design grid is then a six by nine-inch rectangle. You may want to trace this grid onto your border with a removeable marker.

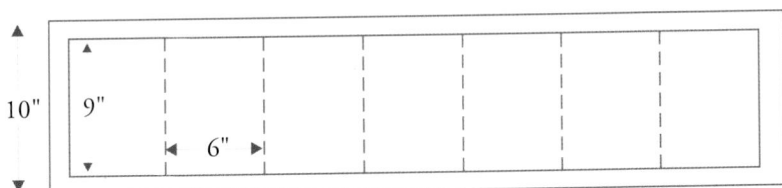

These measurements show your border design area on a ten-inch border. You can trace this grid onto your border with a removeable marker.

You can also make yourself a six or twelve-inch grid by folding and pressing your border strips accordian fashion, leaving a visible line. You can then place your vine and appliqué pieces freehand, using the fold-lines as a guide.

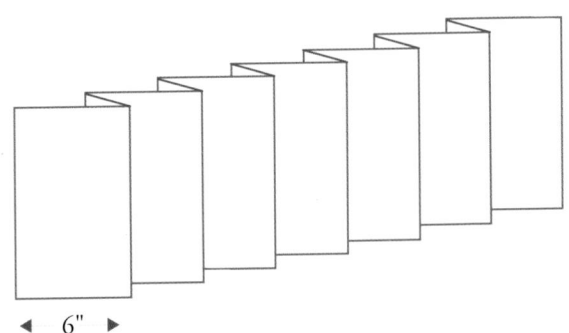

You can also fold your border strip, accordian fashion, leaving a visible fold line to follow when placing your vine and appliqué pieces.

Placing and Sewing the Appliqué

Because I machine-appliqué, I always appliqué most of my border (not including corners) before I attach the border to the quilt. I also think this works best for hand-appliqué.

Fold your border strips in half lengthwise, to mark the center. Press. Fold widthwise to mark the middle of the border lengths. Using a removeable marker, sketch the curve and the corners. Begin by placing your vine – starting in the middle of each border strip and working

25

towards the end – pinning, basting or glueing with water-soluble glue as you go. Glue down the bias to within a few inches of the corner, and be sure to leave extra length so you can curve your corners later, after you have stitched the appliquéd borders to the quilt's center.

Appliqué the vine, leaving the corner ends loose.

Next, place birds, flowers and leaves/cones on your vine (not including the corners). Remember, you don't want your motifs too close to the seam allowance, so place them within the nine-inch design area noted above. If the leaves are too big, overlap the vine or try another angle. Secure them with basting, glue or pins. If you are using stems, you will want to insert them now.

Appliqué birds, leaves/cones, flowers (and stems if you have them), all except the corner leaves and flowers. Leave the corners unsewn for the moment.

Border Corners

I find it easiest to leave the corners for the last step. Sew the borders to the quilt, mitering the corner. (Remove the basted or glued corner appliqué as you need to.) Now take the extra length of vine bias at the end of each border and curve it to make your corner turn. Finally, place, baste and sew the corner flowers and leaves. Depending on whether you're using a relaxed or tight border curve, you should have a relaxed or tight border corner.

Making the Border Your Own - Not Designing on the Computer

If you feel comfortable in doing a little of your own designing, you can use the CD to print out border motifs to make a unique quilt, without designing it on the computer. Patti Butcher, in her *Oklahoma* quilt (fig. 5), included corners of two crossed vines for an original touch. You can always add more birds, flowers and leaves if you think things are too sparse. The palmetto leaf is bigger and more interesting than the elm leaf, and looks great by itself. But if your elm or magnolia leaves look isolated, you may want to scatter more of the simple leaves. You could also arrange the simple leaves in a pattern to add more detail (fig. 6).

fig. 5: Oklahoma, page 116.

The birds, flowers and leaves can be modified. Sharon Vesecky (fig. 7) and bobbi frances mcdonald (fig. 8) both used a three-dimensional appliqué technique for the floral designs in their quilts, *Mississippi* and *New Yawk! New Yawk!*. Shauna Christensen (fig. 9), in her *California Families* quilt, reduced the quail design on the

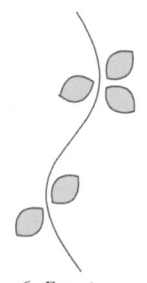

fig. 6: Experiment with leaf placement until you find a look you like.

photocopy machine and made a parade of Mama quail and chicks. On her *Home is Where…* ♥ quilt (fig. 10), Shauna ignored the nine-inch boundary on the borders and overlapped her leaves and birds onto the pieced center. That design trick – letting the border trespass into the center – works well with simple blocks.

And you can always use fewer birds, flowers or leaves and cones if you think the design is too busy or crowded. I appliquéd nothing but leaves on the vine of my *Rolling Stone* (fig. 11). With eleven states to represent, I realized I'd have far too many flowers and birds to fit in the border of one quilt. Pamela Mayfield, in her *Hawaii* quilt (fig. 12), decided against using the Nene (goose), so her border is a graceful combination of kukui leaves and hibiscus framing a delicate appliqué. The Nene, cute as he is, would have looked like a goose in a china shop.

Adding Detail with Ink or Embroidery

If you feel that your birds need eyes, the best way to add them is with a little embroidery. Use a French knot or a few satin stitches. Inking with a waterproof fabric marker is also very effective. You can even stitch some feet on the birds if you think they're needed. The California quail's little curlique top knot is a must (fig. 13). Shauna Christensen embroidered hers. You can also embroider or ink pine needles onto your pine cones for added realism (fig. 14).

Hand Quilting

There are too many possible state patterns to go into detail about quilting designs for your pieced quilt center. The borders are similar enough, however, that I can make some

fig. 7: Sharon Vesecky, Mississippi, page 88.

fig. 8: bobbi frances mcdonald, New Yawk! New Yawk!, page 106.

fig. 9: Shauna Christensen, California Families, page 42.

fig. 10: Shauna Christensen, Home is Where… ♥, page 138.

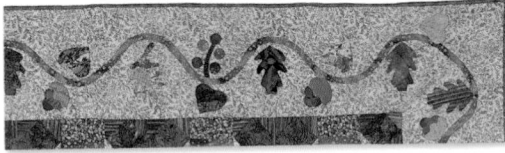

fig. 11: Barbara Brackman, Rolling Stone, page 158.

fig. 12: Pamela Mayfield, Hawaii, page 58.

fig 13: Embroider or ink the quail's plume.

suggestions drawn from my study of some of the best 1930s quilts. For the leaves, quilt a vein down the middle – that is if your state leaf has a vein down the middle (fig. 15). For flowers with a central color area, you might quilt a circle or other shape right in the middle (fig. 16). For birds, quilt lines indicating feathers in the wings or tail, or lines down the middle of each wing (fig. 17). It's not necessary to do any more quilting inside birds, cones, flowers and leaves of this size. You are better off leaving the motif relatively unquilted, and just outlining the appliqué about ¼" away from the edge.

The quilt artists of the 1930s did a lot of filler-quilting behind the appliqué motifs. You may want to try a diagonal line or a diagonal grid. Or, if you want to do twice as much quilting, stitch a double-diagonal line or double grid (fig. 18). These filler lines should stop at the appliqué outline and not go across the leaf or bird. You can also continue the outlines around the appliqué motifs by echoing in concentric lines. I wouldn't bother with cables, feathers or any kind of fancy designs unless you've left a lot of light-colored area as Susannah Christenson did in her *Virginia* quilt on page 142. Fancy quilting motifs just don't show up well on prints or dark shades.

Machine Quilting

Many of the quilts in the book were machine-quilted by Pamela Mayfield. Pamela does free-hand design using her sewing machine, a variety of feet, and colored polyester or cotton sewing thread that she chooses with a good eye for color. On her own *Hawaii* quilt, she drew freehand floral shapes in the hibiscus as she stitched. She put leafy shapes in the leaves, and meander-quilted around the appliqué, to fill in the background. For my *Rolling Stone*, she quilted a double

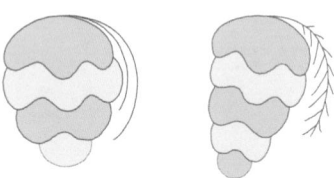

fig. 14: Choose the best needles.
Ink or embroider.

fig. 15: Left: Kukui leaf with machine quilting.
Right: Redbud leaf with hand quilting.

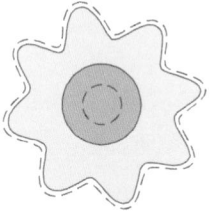

fig. 16: Sunflower with hand quilting.

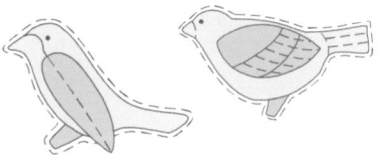

fig. 17: Left: Brown Thrasher for Georgia with simple quilting and inked eye. Right: Lark Bunting for Colorado with a satin-stitch eye and quilted feathers.

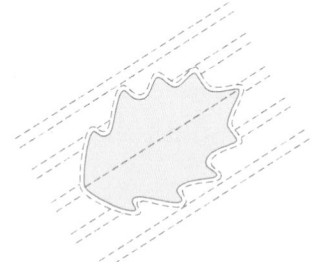

fig. 18: Hand quilting with a double-diagonal line as filler.

diagonal line in the border, stitching right over the leaves and vines. For Jean Stanclift's *Kansas,* she outlined each appliqué motif right on the seam line, then echoed that outline in rows of stitches 1/4" apart (fig. 19).

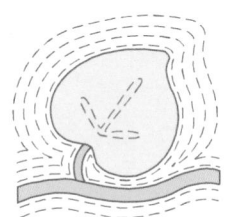

fig. 19: Machine quilting using an outline and echo.

Cutting and Making Bias Strips

Using a Bias Tape Maker

I use a bias tape maker, a little metal tool that costs about $3. They come in a variety of sizes. For this quilt 1/2" works well.

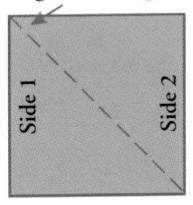

Diagonal cutting line

Side 1   Side 2

fig. 20: Cut a 20-inch square diagonally.

Cut strips diagonally across your fabric. Cut the strips twice as wide as you want the finished strip to be. For a 1/2" wide vine, cut 1" strips.

Thread the bias strip through the bias tape maker tool. The bias strip will automatically be folded the right size. Steam-press the strip as it comes out of the bias tape maker. Store your folded bias strips on a tube (I use an old paper towel core), so they stay folded.

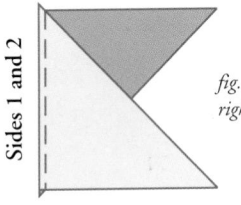

Sides 1 and 2

fig. 21: Sew the pieces right sides together.

Using a Continuous Bias Method

Cut a square or a rectangle about 20" wide. Cut a line on the bias across the rectangle (fig. 20). Using a 1/4" seam allowance, sew the pieces right sides together (fig. 21). Press that seam open. Draw lines 1" apart on this parallelogram (fig. 22).

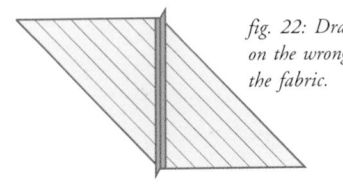

fig. 22: Draw lines on the wrong side of the fabric.

Stitch the parallelogram into a tube by bringing the bias edges together, with the right sides together. Offset the edges however, lining up the second line with the first one (fig. 23). Machine-stitch this seam. Press the seam open.

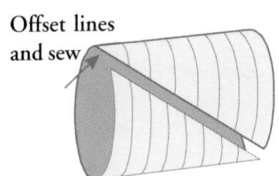

Offset lines and sew

fig. 23: Stitch the parallelogram into a tube matching the second line with the first line.

Using scissors, cut along the lines in a continuous cut and you will have several yards of bias which you can fold into 1/2" strips (fig. 24).

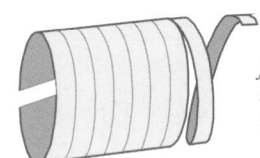

fig. 24: Cut along the lines to create bias strips.

Alabama

Heart of Dixie

Alabama, "The Heart of Dixie," has a long quiltmaking tradition.
Naturally, Alabama quilters named patterns
to honor their state.

When *Hearth & Home* magazine printed a pattern for every state during the first decade of last century, their **Alabama** entry was a classic nine-patch variation. Note its similarity to

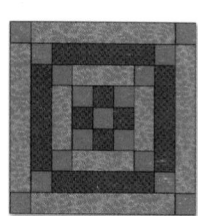

Alabama

Alabama Rambler, a pattern from a 1930's *Chicago Tribune* Nancy Cabot column. Nancy said it was popular in an earlier time, made in reds and greens to represent roses and leaves.

The Cabot column also included an **Alabama Beauty** (a) (known also as Tobacco Leaf), which makes a striking all-over pattern. The Aunt Martha Studios

sold a second **Alabama Beauty** (b) pattern – a prizewinning entry by a Hamilton, Alabama, woman – in Aunt Martha's block contest of the early '30s.

Mountain Mist patterns, from the Stearns & Foster Company (now called the Stearns Technical Textiles Company), named the classic diamond star pattern **Stars of Alabama** after the

*Scenes of Mobile
include public buildings
and the bay in a card
mailed in 1944.*

Alabama Rambler   Alabama Beauty (a)   Alabama Beauty (b)

Stars of Alabama   Cotton Reels   LeMoyne Star

Montgomery   Southern Star   Southern Pine

Cotton State. To honor Alabama's most famous crop, I have included **Cotton Reels** from *All About Patchwork*, a Golden Hands Publication.

The Thorny Thicket

Like many states, Alabama's lyrical name is derived from the native Indian language. Early French settlers named a river after the Alibamons, a tribe whose Choctaw name meant "thicket clearers" or "cultivators." We can remember those native Alabamans with **The Thorny Thicket** from the *Kansas City Star* quilt column of August 5, 1942.

French settlers were headed by Pierre and Jean Baptiste LeMoyne, a name familiar to quilt pattern collectors. The LeMoyne brothers sailed from Canada to claim southern lands for France in the early 1700s. They founded the first permanent European settlement in Alabama near Mobile, and later founded New Orleans, for which they are better known. Ruth Finley tells the story of the **LeMoyne Star** in her 1929 book, *Old Patchwork Quilts and the Women Who Made Them.*

When Alabama became the 22nd state in 1819, its capital was Montgomery. The Confederacy was later founded at Montgomery in February, 1861. *Hearth & Home's* **Montgomery** block honors that city.

The Alabama state tree is the Southern Pine. Alice Brooks sold a **Southern Pine** pattern in her 1930's syndicated column. Since Alabama is the "Heart of Dixie," a **Southern Belle** from Clara A.

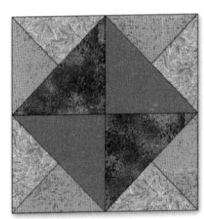

Southern Belle

Stone's 1906 *Practical Needlework: Quilt Patterns* or a **Southern Star** from Grandma Dexter, another 1930s pattern source, are good choices for an Alabama quilt.

Camellia

Southern Pine Cone

Yellowhammer

State facts about...
Alabama

Date Entered Union:	**December 14, 1819**
Order of Admission:	**22**
State Capital:	**Montgomery**
State Flower:	**Camellia**
State Bird:	**Yellowhammer**
State Tree:	**Southern pine**
Nickname:	**Heart of Dixie**
Motto:	***Audemus jura nostra defendere***
	(We dare defend our rights)

Alaska

The Last Frontier

Alaska's state flag, with eight golden stars on a midnight-blue field,
symbolizes the state's mineral resources and the northern skies. I found
eight stars for an Alaskan quilt and a few other patterns
to represent "America's Last Frontier."

Our largest state is also one of the newest. It became the 49th state in 1959. Yet, surprisingly, by the early 1900s, Alaska already had a pattern named for it. The block appeared in *Hearth and Home* magazine's series of state quilt patterns submitted by readers. The reason? The block **Alaska** originally

Alaska

honored the territory, since the magazine asked readers to submit patterns for territories as well as states. The same magazine requested capital city patterns too. At the time, **Sitka** was the territorial capital. And that's the reason that Sitka has a quilt pattern, while Juneau, today's state capital, has none I could find.

Early Russian explorers recorded the native people's name for the land. Spelled in a variety of ways – from Alesksu to Alaxsxag – the word roughly translates: Mainland. When Russia sold the land

Cantilever bridge, 215 feet high, on the White Pass and Yukon Railroad.

32

Sitka

The North Star

Polaris Star

Pole Star

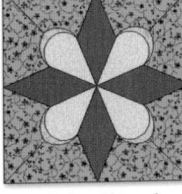
Alaska Chinook

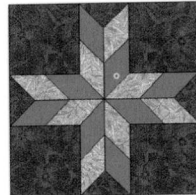
Fish Tails

to the United States in 1867, Secretary of State, William Seward bought it for a few pennies an acre. Skeptics, doubting it was worth even that, called it "Seward's Folly" and "Seward's Icebox" until gold was discovered.

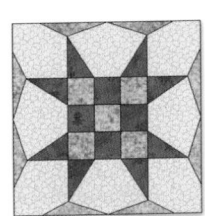
Klondike Star

The Klondike gold rush began in 1896 and continued into the early twentieth century. Remember the gold rush with **Klondike Star**, a pattern in Clara Stone's quilt pattern catalog, published in 1906, when Alaska's first boom towns were still booming.

Big Dipper

The territorial flag was adopted in 1927. The stars represent the North Star and the Big Dipper. Include a **Big Dipper** in your Alaskan sampler. This pattern, one of patchwork's oldest, was recorded in the Ladies Art Company catalog at the end of the nineteenth century. **The North Star**, from a 1949 *Kansas City Star*, can

represent the flag's large corner star. Or consider **Polaris Star** or **Pole Star**, two other names for the North Star. Polaris Star is from Carrie Hall's 1935 book, *The Romance of the Patchwork Quilt in America*. Pole Star appeared in *The American Woman* magazine around 1920.

An outstanding feature of the Alaskan sky is the **Northern Lights**, a pattern from the Nancy Page column syndicated in 1930's newspapers around the United States. **Alaska Chinook**, from the Nancy Cabot column in the *Chicago Tribune* at the same time, was named for the warm winds that melt the winter snow.

Northern Lights

Alaska's official state fish is the King Salmon – so **Fish Tails**, another star design from Clara Stone, is perfect for "The Land of the Midnight Sun."

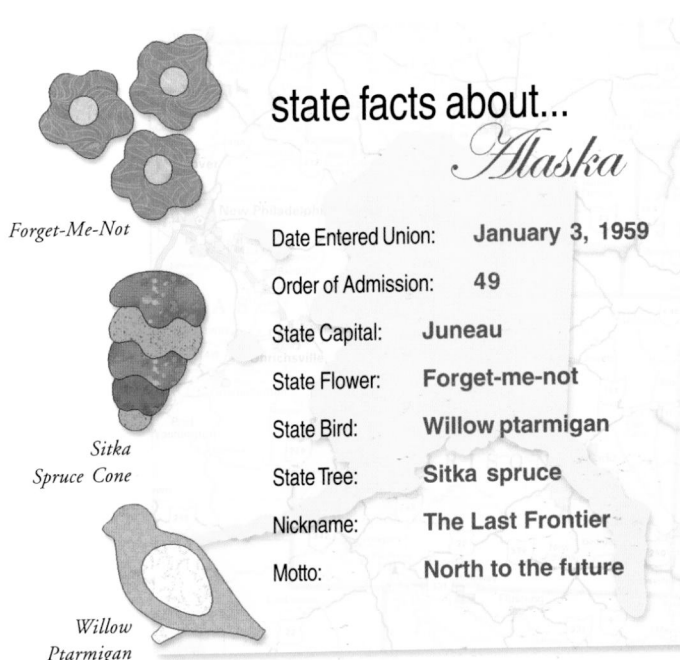
Forget-Me-Not

Sitka Spruce Cone

Willow Ptarmigan

state facts about...
Alaska

Date Entered Union:	**January 3, 1959**
Order of Admission:	**49**
State Capital:	**Juneau**
State Flower:	**Forget-me-not**
State Bird:	**Willow ptarmigan**
State Tree:	**Sitka spruce**
Nickname:	**The Last Frontier**
Motto:	**North to the future**

Arizona

Grand Canyon State

Poet Stephen Vincent Benét once wrote that he had fallen in love
with American names like Tucson and Deadwood and Lost Mule Flat.
Many of us have the same feeling about quilt pattern names. Some patterns named
for Arizona, its history or its geography – like Prickly Pear, Cactus Basket and Apache
Trail – have the same poetic power Benét loved.

Arizona is the Spanish version of an Indian word meaning "little spring." The original Indian place called Arizona remained part of Mexico as the territory's borders changed several times over the course of settlement. But the U.S. Congress liked the sound of "Arizona" and chose it for the territory, and later the state, when it became the 48th star on the flag in 1912.

State of Arizona

About that time *Hearth and Home* magazine asked readers to submit quilt patterns for each state and territory. As a result, the block **State of Arizona** was published some time around 1910. The Nancy Page column published a second **Arizona** pattern in the 1930s. *Hearth and Home* also asked readers for patterns honoring state capitals, so **Phoenix** was pictured in that magazine.

In the Spring every native tree and plant bursts into bloom, transforming the desert into a carpet of rainbow hue.

Arizona's first settlers, the Indians, have profoundly influenced the state's culture. Many Arizona-related quilt patterns reflect an Indian design influence, or what Eastern newspaper editors and designers believed to be an Indian look. Of the state's many tribes, only two – the Apache and Navajo – seem to have quilt patterns named specifically for them.

Apache Trail

Apache Trail was shown in the *Chicago Tribune's* Nancy Cabot column in 1938. Variations on **Navajo** have appeared in Mountain Mist pattern catalogs since 1928.

Much of Arizona came under U.S. domination in 1848 after the war with Mexico, a victory celebrated by many seamstresses with lovely Mexican Rose applique quilts. The pattern seems to be one of the few authentic politically inspired quilt designs. Today we find so many carefully preserved Mexican Rose

Arizona — *Phoenix* — *Navajo*

Mexican Rose — *Letha's Electric Fan* — *Prickly Pear (b)*

Cactus Flower — *Arizona's Cactus Flower* — *Cactus Rose*

quilts made in the late 1840s and 1850s that it is easy to believe that women's quilts of the time expressed their support of United States territorial expansion. Remember this war with a pieced **Mexican Rose** block, also known as Mexican Star.

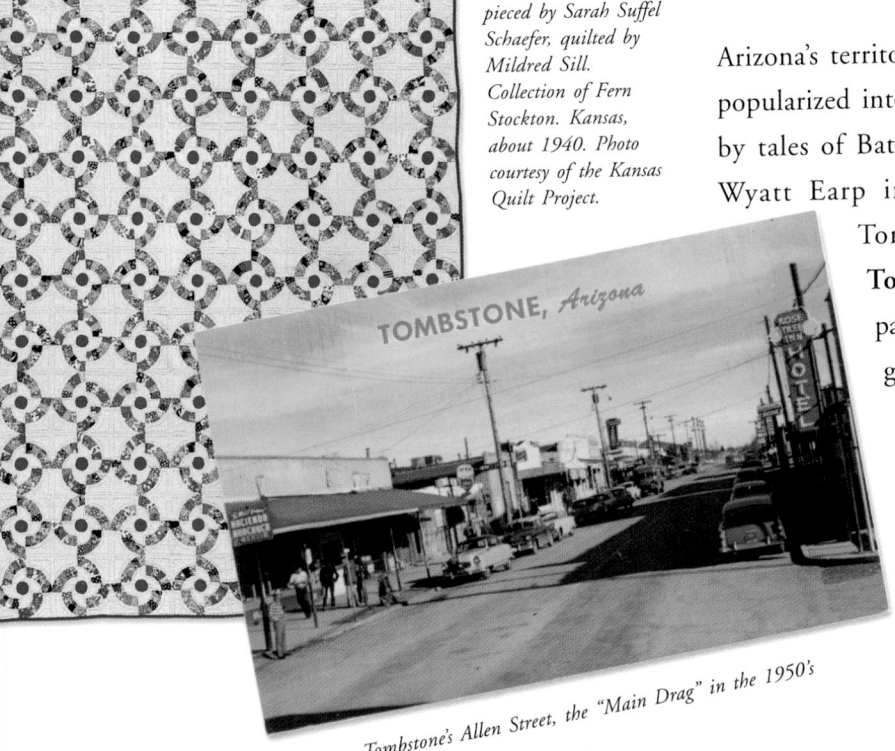

Letha's Electric Fan, pieced by Sarah Suffel Schaefer, quilted by Mildred Sill. Collection of Fern Stockton. Kansas, about 1940. Photo courtesy of the Kansas Quilt Project.

TOMBSTONE, Arizona

Tombstone's Allen Street, the "Main Drag" in the 1950's

Arizona's territorial history was popularized into national myth by tales of Bat Masterson and Wyatt Earp in the town of Tombstone. The **Tombstone Quilt**

Tombstone Quilt

pattern commemorates these cowboys, gunfighters, and boomtowns.

Arizona's current vitality as a sunbelt state is due both to the desert sun that warms its winters and to modern cooling systems that cool homes and offices in summers.

State facts about...
Arizona

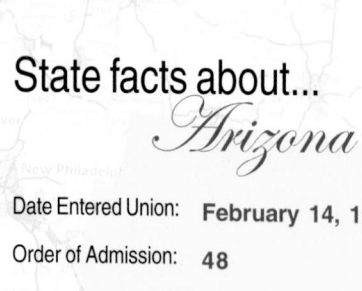

Date Entered Union: **February 14, 1912**

Order of Admission: **48**

State Capital: **Phoenix**

State Flower: **Saguaro cactus blossom**

State Bird: **Cactus wren**

State Tree: **Paloverde**

Nickname: **Grand Canyon State**

Motto: ***Diat Deus*** **(God enriches)**

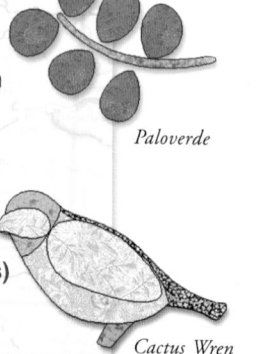

Saguaro Cactus Blossom

Paloverde

Cactus Wren

The Grand Canyon is a mile deep in places.

Sunbeam

For the winter sun you might include **Sunbeam** in an Arizona sampler. The pattern is from Ruby Short McKim's *101 Patchwork Patterns* from the 1930s. For the summer breeze, how about **Letha's Electric Fan**, an Art Deco variation on an old favorite from a 1938 *Kansas City Star*.

Cactus Basket

Many designs represent Arizona's striking desert vegetation. While no pattern is specifically named for the saguaro cactus, **Cactus Basket**, from Ruth Finley's *Old Patchwork Quilts and the Women Who Made Them*, or **Cactus Rose**, could represent the state flower. The latter design was a popular mid-nineteenth century pattern, also called The Lily. The Shelburne Museum and the American Museum in Britain call their examples Cactus Rose.

Prickly Pear is a cactus with two patterns named for it: one is from Ruth Finley's book (a); the other is a 1931 *Kansas City Star* design (b). The same year the *Kansas City Star* pictured a **Cactus Flower**. And in 1935 *Workbasket* magazine showed four of these blocks set together as **Arizona's Cactus Flower** in the All-State Quilt their artists designed.

Prickly Pear cactus in a garden of western native plants

Prickly Pear (a)

36

Arkansas

The Natural State

Arkansas is a rural state, best known for its Ozark Mountains, folkways and folk arts, including quilts. The abundance of Arkansas-related quilt patterns shows quiltmaking's vitality in the state.

The state's name comes from the French settlers who included the area in the Louisiana Purchase. Congress named it Arkansaw when they made it a territory in 1819. Over the years, people began spelling it with a final "s," but continued pronouncing it Arkansaw, as in the early spelling. By the mid-nineteenth century, pronouncing and spelling the state's name became such an issue that the Vice-President, presiding over the Senate, called one of the state's senators the "Senator from Ar'kansaw," the other the "Senator from Arkan'sas."

Arkansas (a)

Hearth and Home magazine published their version of **Arkansas** (a) in the early twentieth century. The magazine also published **Little Rock**, named after the state capital.

In 1951, Dick sent this card to his grandma. "We are zooming along at 70 m.p.h. in the heart of Arkansas. We have been riding in cotton for about one hour."

The Arkansas Traveler, a popular fiddle tune, gives its name to several patterns. **Arkansas Traveler** (a) appeared in the Ladies Art Company catalog published in the late nineteenth century. Ruth Finley showed another **Arkansas Traveler** (b) in her 1929 book *Old Patchwork Quilts and the Women Who Made Them*. And Carrie Hall pictured yet another **Arkansas Traveler** (c) in *The Romance of the Patchwork Quilt in America*, published in 1935.

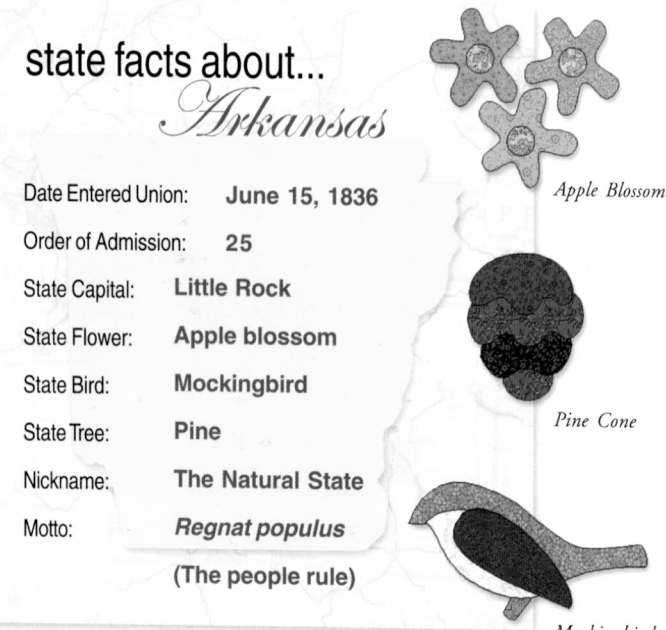

Arkansas Star (a)

The *Kansas City Star*, which published a regional Arkansas edition, is an important source for Arkansas- named patterns. This newspaper, which had an edition known as the *Weekly Star Farmer*, printed patterns

Arkansas Traveler (a) *Arkansas Traveler (b)* *Arkansas Traveler (c)*

Arkansas Troubles *Arkansas (b)* *Arkansas Centennial*

Arkansas Meadow Rose *Arkansas Cross Roads* *Arkansas Star (b)*

Ozark Cobblestones *Ozark Diamonds* *Little Rock*

by staff artists and reader contributors. **Ozark Diamonds** or Ozark Star was by the *Kansas City Star's* designer Eveline Foland. **Arkansas Star** (a) and **Arkansas** (b) were originally drawn by their Edna Marie Dunn. **Arkansas Meadow Rose**, **Arkansas Centennial**, **Arkansas Cross Roads**, and Arkansas Snow Flake, also called **Arkansas Star** (b), are *Star* reader contributions.

Ozark Cobblestones is a Ladies Art Company pattern originally named Octagon, but renamed after the mountain range by an Arkansas quilter proud of her home. *Workbasket* magazine's All-State Quilt sampler in the 1930s featured **Arkansas Troubles**.

California

Golden State

California has long been viewed as the Promised Land.
So it is not surprising that the road to California has been
commemorated in quilt designs.

In their late-nineteenth-century catalog, the Ladies Art Company included a **Road to California** (a) block, which seems to represent a journey made up of countless small steps. A second

version of **Road to California** (b) from Carlie Sexton, who had an Illinois mail-order pattern company in the 1930s, includes one set with alternating plain blocks. Another **Road to California** (c) came from the Missouri pattern company run by Ruby S. McKim. (This last pattern was also called Off to

Road to California (c)

San Francisco in the widely syndicated Nancy Page newspaper column.) A variation is **Rocky Road to California** (a) from the Ladies Art Company catalog of the 1890s. Another **Rocky Road to California** (b) appeared in Carrie Hall's 1935 book, *The Romance of the Patchwork Quilt in America*. (This block

Romance on the desert

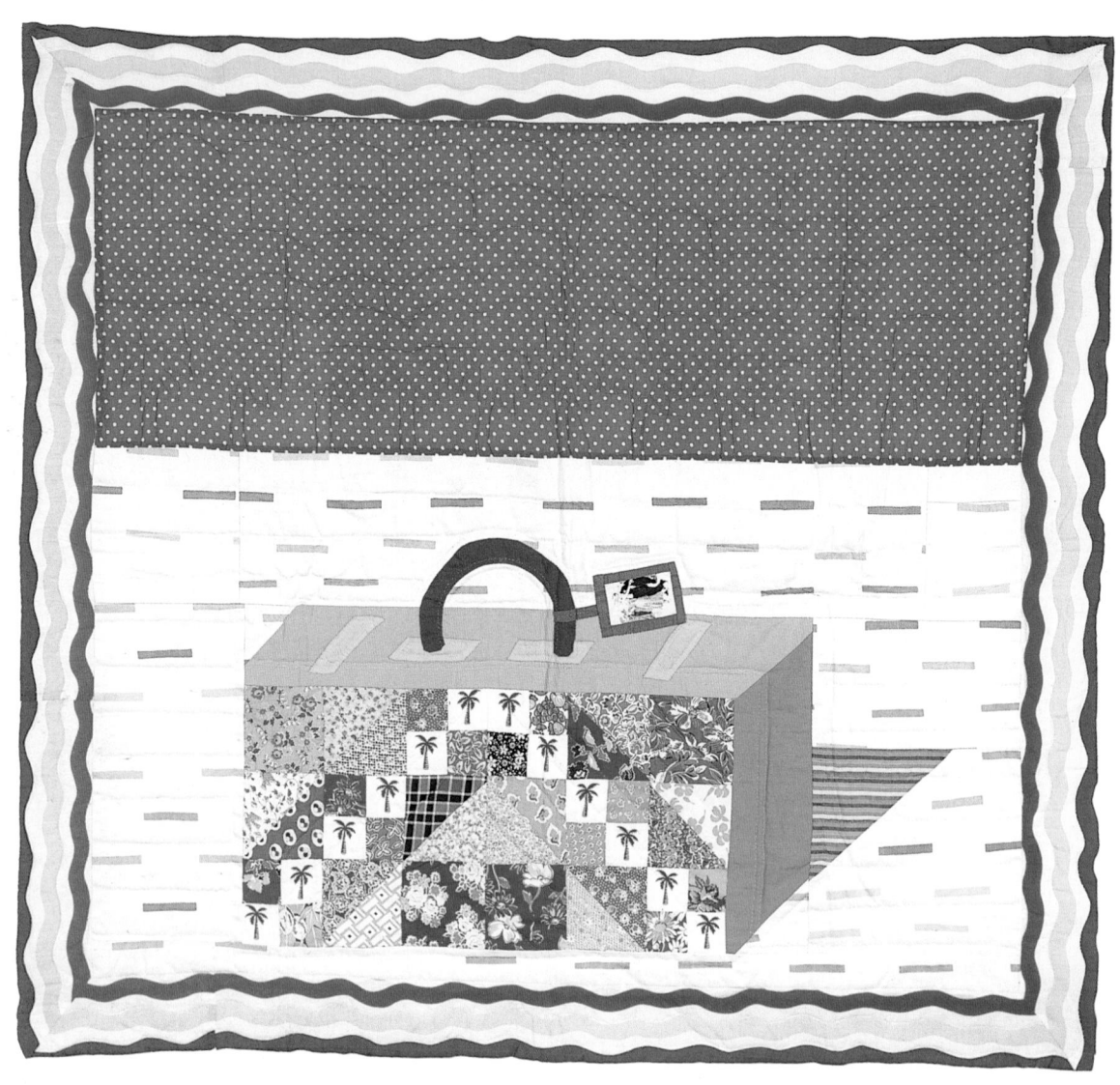

The Road to California

by Barbara Brackman, Lawrence, Kansas, 1990.
I used the traditional Road to California pattern in this homage to Hollywood,
made from antique and new fabrics.

Journey to California

is better known as Drunkard's Path to most quiltmakers.) And a **Journey to California** in a 1955 issue of the *Weekly Kansas City Star* was a new name for the old Snail's Trail design.

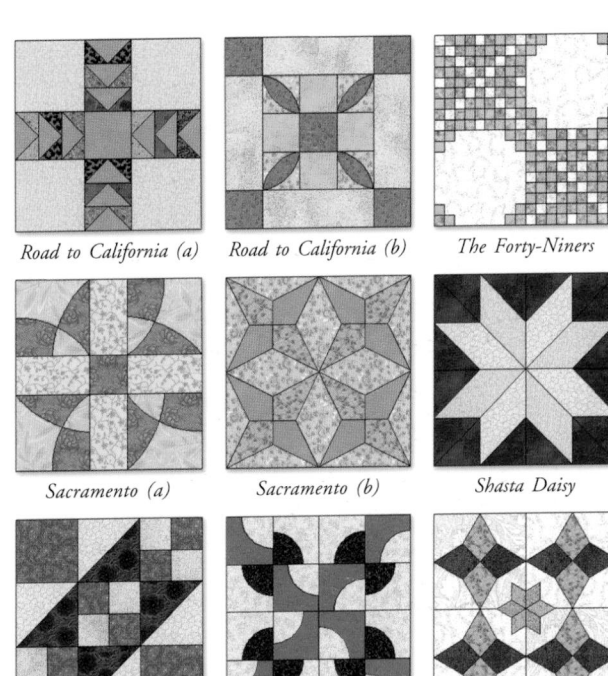

Road to California (a)

Road to California (b)

The Forty-Niners

Sacramento (a)

Sacramento (b)

Shasta Daisy

Rocky Road to California (a)

Rocky Road to California (b)

Hollywood

We catch a glimpse of how rocky the road really was by reading diaries and letters of the women who traveled westward with the wagon trains. Kenneth L. Holmes' series, *Covered Wagon Women* (University of Nebraska Press, 1997), has published dozens of first-person accounts like that of Mariett Foster Cummings. Cummings walked the road to California from Illinois in 1852, when she was 25 years old. On Friday the 13th of August, her party came within sight of California. "We have been four long months today on this journey. I am sick and oh how weak." The next day the discouraged traveler wrote in her diary: "two miles brought us to the summit of the Sierra Nevada mountains. I walked a few rods and feebly did my feet press California soil for the first time. The goal of my ambition…" Although Mariett feared she might die on the trip, she lived a long and prosperous life in San Jose and San Francisco.

The name California is one of the oldest recorded American place names. According to George R. Stewart's book, *Names on the Land*, sixteenth-century Spanish explorers had heard of an island inhabited only by women where the footpaths were of gold and pearls. Sailors, discovering the

California (a)

tip of a long peninsula in the Pacific, hoped it might be some kind of earthly paradise. The **California** (a) quilt pattern named for this paradise is from *Hearth and Home* magazine's state quilt block pattern series, published around 1910. The Nancy Page syndicated newspaper quilt column of the 1930s published a

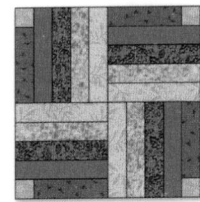

California (b)

simple **California** (b) block. Both blocks form interwoven designs when repeated.

"Against the growing desert sunset, the grotesque Joshua tree spreads its shaggy branches. Many desert birds nest in these spiny trees and Indians use the small roots for basket weaving."

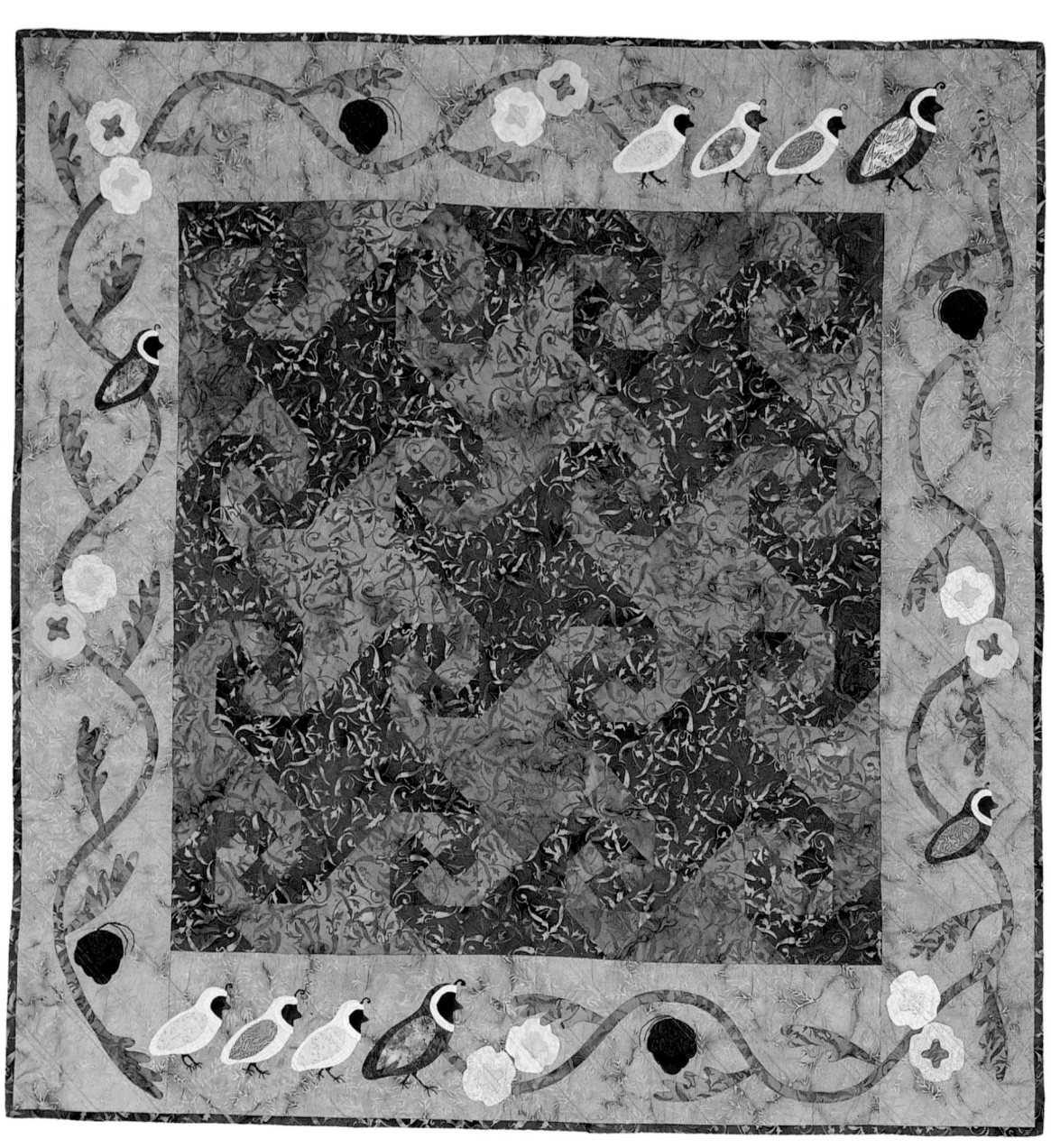

California Families

by Shauna O. Christensen, Lawrence, Kansas, 2001.
Machine-pieced and appliquéd by Shauna Christensen. Machine-quilted by Pamela Mayfield.
Shauna repeated the center of the Journey to California block to make her own pieced quilt center. In the border she created
quail families by making some of the quail smaller. Her vine also holds golden poppies,
California redwood cones and her own poppy leaf design.

When in the Golden State, every tourist wants to see a California "star." In quilt patterns a California Star is a feathered star with a nine-patch center. The Ladies Art Company from St. Louis showed a **California Star** (a) in their late-nineteenth-century catalog. And *Aunt Kate's Quilting Bee* magazine from the 1960s drew a **California Star** (b) variation. Carrie Hall added more stars to the Nine-Patch and came up with a superstar in her **California Star** (c).

California Star, by Letha Rice, Leavenworth, Kansas, about 1970.

California Star (a)

California Star (b)

California Star (c)

When Ruby McKim designed her *Patchwork Parade of States* in the 1930s she chose a variation of the Irish Chain design to represent the gold miners of California. **The Forty-Niners** block alternates a block pieced of 49 squares. Many women came with the miners. Elizabeth Keegan wasn't pleased with the company she met in the mining towns. Soon after her arrival in 1852, she wrote a homesick letter to her brother and sister back in St. Louis. "Society is at a very low ebb though I must say there are some families here of the highest respectability, but they keep no company....One word to young ladies who are aspiring, that if they wish to be comfortable and enjoy society they had better stay where they are." Despite her complaints, she knew she'd made the right choice in traveling the California road. "The wealth of mines could not purchase me to return."

Pattern designers have also honored a few California cities. The state capital can claim **Sacramento** (a&b), both from *Hearth and Home* magazine. Mariposa, a city near Yosemite National Park, has **Mariposa Lily** according to Carrie Hall. Shasta – a city, a mountain, a lake and a daisy – inspired **Shasta Daisy** from the Laura Wheeler syndicated newspaper column. **Hollywood** is from Mountain Mist patterns which advertised the design in 1935 as "daringly modern."

Mariposa Lily

State facts about...
California

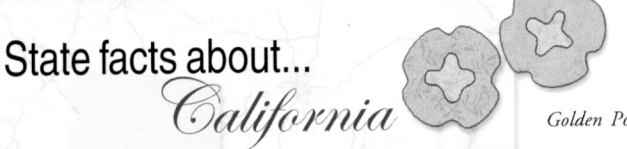

Golden Poppies

California Redwood Cone

California Valley Quail

Date Entered Union:	September 9, 1850
Order of Admission:	31
State Capital:	Sacramento
State Flower:	Golden poppy
State Bird:	California quail
State Tree:	California redwood
Nickname:	Golden State
Motto:	Eureka! (I have found it!)

Colorado

Colorado's natural beauty and dramatic history
have inspired artists in media from painting to pop music.
Quiltmaking is no exception.

Colorado was the block design chosen by the editors of *Hearth and Home* magazine to represent the state in the early 1900s. Mrs. H.B.W. submitted this six pointed star, noting it was also 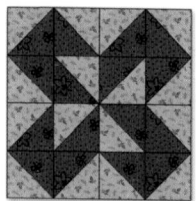 called "Rising Sun." **Colorado Beauty** appeared in *Comfort* magazine about the same time. Kansan Pearl Bacon sent a similar pattern, called **The Colorado Quilt**, to the *Kansas City Star* in

The Colorado Quilt

1941. She'd probably seen the earlier design in *Comfort*; many *Kansas City Star* designs were variations of patterns from earlier magazines.

The name Colorado comes from the river running through the state, named by early Spanish explorers for its red color. These early explorers found many Native Americans living on the land. The native tribes were remembered in 1935 when *Workbasket* magazine published a **Colorado's Arrowhead** pattern in their All-State Quilt, renaming an old pattern for Colorado.

Much of our western land came under U.S. authority through the Louisiana Purchase in 1803. Soon after buying the territory, President Thomas Jefferson sent Army officer Zebulon Pike to

Pikes Peak

survey the purchase. Pike left his mark on Pikes Peak, and his and other explorers' stories of the magnificent landscape captured the fancy of

Colorado

Rocky Mountain Puzzle

Colorado's Arrowhead

Rocky Mountain

Springtime in the Rockies

Silver and Gold

Railroad Around Rocky Mountain

Colorado Beauty

Centennial

through snow. About 1920, **Railroad Around Rocky Mountain** was sent to the *Woman's Century* magazine. And the *Chicago Tribune's* Nancy Cabot column published **Rocky Mountain Puzzle** in the 1930s.

The Rocky Mountain gold rush faded away, but mining remained an important Colorado industry. To honor the miners you can include **Silver and Gold** from the *Kansas City Star*.

Cherry Creek changed its name to **Denver** and the capital city's pattern was included in *Hearth and Home's* state capital pattern series. Colorado became the 38th state in 1876, during America's Centennial celebration, so the state's nickname is the Centennial State. **Centennial** was

Denver

possibly drawn from a quilt exhibited at the Centennial Exposition in Philadelphia, or perhaps designed to commemorate the fair or anniversary. The name was first printed in the 1898 catalog for the Ladies Art Company of St. Louis.

nineteenth-century Americans, including quiltmakers. **Pikes Peak** found its way into Bostonian Clara Stone's 1906 booklet *Practical Needlework Patterns*.

Colorado's hold on the American imagination tightened when gold was discovered near Cherry Creek in 1858. While men rushed off to find their fortunes in the Rockies, women showed off their piecing skills with the **Rocky Mountain** pattern. Today we call this design New York Beauty because Mountain Mist has been selling the pattern under that name since the 1930s. But in the nineteenth century, when so many quilts of this pattern were made, the design was more associated with the western Rockies than New York. Variations of this pattern all have corner quarter-circles; most include sharp pieced triangles in the sashing. But sometimes the set included a serpentine vine, appliquéd or pieced. In 1931, *Capper's Weekly* showed a variation called **Springtime in the Rockies**, recommending green and white to symbolize new grass peeking

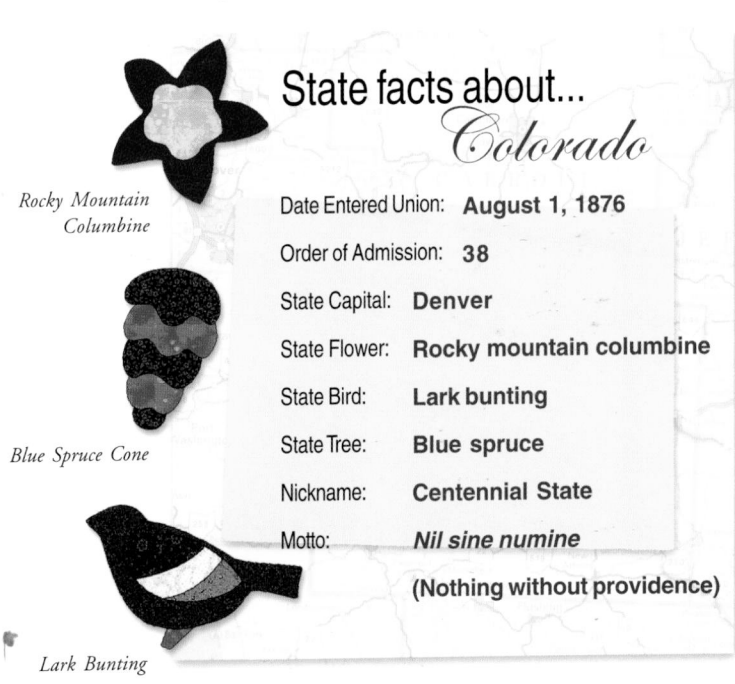

Rocky Mountain Columbine

Blue Spruce Cone

Lark Bunting

State facts about...
Colorado

Date Entered Union:	**August 1, 1876**
Order of Admission:	**38**
State Capital:	**Denver**
State Flower:	**Rocky mountain columbine**
State Bird:	**Lark bunting**
State Tree:	**Blue spruce**
Nickname:	**Centennial State**
Motto:	***Nil sine numine***
	(Nothing without providence)

Connecticut
The Constitution State

As one of the thirteen original colonies, Connecticut has a
quiltmaking tradition dating back to the whole-cloth quilt era in pre-Revolutionary,
pre-patchwork days. Surprisingly, given the state's long quilting history, the search
for state patterns is not as fruitful as it is for many newer states.

The number of blocks named for a state seems more related to how many pattern sources (companies, designers and quilt newspaper columns) a state had, rather than how many years quilts were made there. Connecticut thus has fewer patterns than states such as Iowa or Kansas, both home to many pattern sources in the 1930s.

Readers of Comfort Magazine exchanged postcards as well as quilt patterns. In 1908 Mrs. Bensten sent this card to Maude Shelby in Oklahoma.

Connecticut (a) was the pattern *Hearth and Home* magazine selected to represent the state in their state series, published in the first decades of the twentieth century. A second **Connecticut** (b) appeared in the 1930s, in the Nancy Page syndicated newspaper quilt column. A reader from Weston, Connecticut, sent the pattern, writing that she thought it looked "just like the state, neat and tidy." In 1937, *Farm Journal* offered **Connecticut Star** (a variation of a pattern better known as Dove at the Window or Four Birds, because careful shading of the diamonds reveals birds flying toward the block's center).

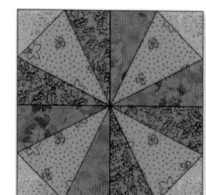

Connecticut (a)

46

The state capital, **Hartford**, was remembered with a pattern in *Hearth and Home's* second pattern series in the years 1912 – 1916, named for state capitals. In 1945, *Farm Journal* published **Hope of Hartford**, an unusual eight-pointed star. The name may relate to a trading post called "The House of Good Hope," an early Dutch settlement near Hartford.

Connecticut's history is represented in several Charter Oak appliqué block designs (not shown). The Charter Oak legend describes how the English King Charles II gave early Connecticut colonists a charter guaranteeing democratic self-government. A later ruler, James II, sent an emissary to seize the charter and take away their rights. But clever colonists kept him waiting through long, windy speeches until after dark. Before he could carry away their charter, the candles were mysteriously snuffed. When the candles were relit, the charter had disappeared, hidden, the story goes, in a large hollow oak. The Charter Oak and its legend remained important symbols throughout the American Revolution and early years of the Republic. In 1856,

Connecticut (b) Connecticut Star Hartford

Hope of Hartford Red Robin Bird's Nest

Yankee Charm New England Block Yankee Pride

the enormous Charter Oak tree blew down in a storm. Today a stone monument stands near the tree's former site, in the city of Hartford. The state tree is the white oak, the same species as the Charter Oak.

The state bird is the American Robin. If you want to include a pieced bird in your Connecticut quilt, there is **Red Robin** from the Laura Wheeler/Alice Brooks newspaper syndicate. Or, you might shade the diamonds in your Connecticut Star a robin's-breast red, or color the small squares in **Bird's Nest** a robin's-egg blue to symbolize the state bird.

To commemorate the Nutmeg state's history and natural beauty, piece **Yankee Charm**, a novel arrangement of traditional quilt design elements that appeared in the *Chicago Tribune's* Nancy Cabot column in the 1930s. The **New England Block** is from the Needlecraft Supply Company. And don't forget **Yankee Pride** from quilt book author, Ruth Finley, who took great pride in her Connecticut ancestry.

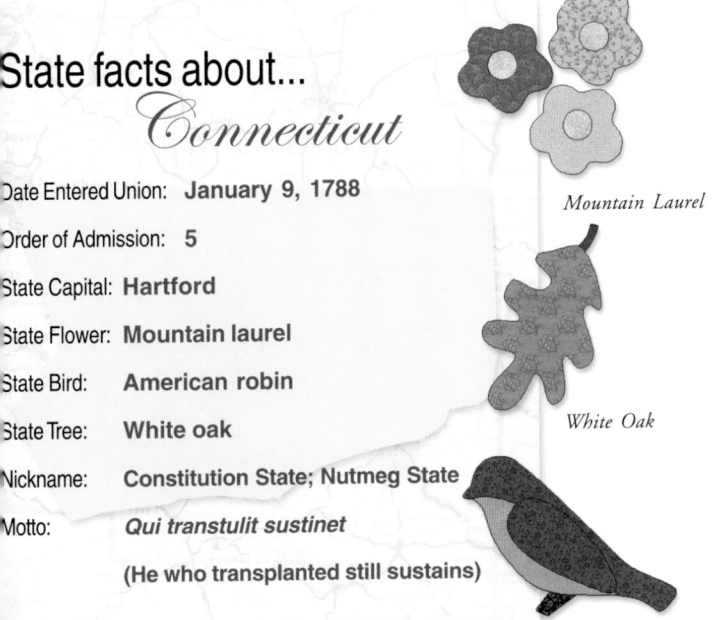

State facts about...
Connecticut

Date Entered Union: **January 9, 1788**

Order of Admission: **5**

State Capital: **Hartford**

State Flower: **Mountain laurel**

State Bird: **American robin**

State Tree: **White oak**

Nickname: **Constitution State; Nutmeg State**

Motto: *Qui transtulit sustinet*

(He who transplanted still sustains)

Mountain Laurel

White Oak

Robin

Delaware

First State

Early explorers named Delaware Bay after Virginia's first governor, Lord De La Warr.
The otherwise forgotten English lord has at least two American rivers,
a state, an Indian tribe (also called the Leni-Lanape)
and several quilt patterns named for him.

The **Delaware** quilt block is from *Hearth and Home* magazine's state block series, printed in the early twentieth century. **Delaware Crosspatch** appeared in a 1930s Nancy Cabot column in the *Chicago Tribune*. About the same time, *Workbasket* magazine designed an All-State Quilt with a Four-Patch made of two separate blocks for Delaware. **Delaware's Flagstones** is one of more than a dozen names for this two-block pattern.

Swedes were the first Europeans to build a permanent settlement, creating a colony called New Sweden. They brought with them a distinctive building style – homes built of rough-hewn logs laid in courses. Two centuries later, the Swedish log cabin is as American as apple pie and patchwork quilts. Commemorate Delaware's early Swedish settlers with a **Log Cabin** (a) block of strips. And don't forget to make the center square red, symbolizing the hearth – the heart of the cabin. For a more realistic Log Cabin, use **Log Cabin** (b) from the Ladies Art Company pattern company, about the turn of the last century.

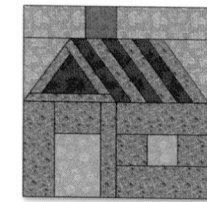

Log Cabin (b)

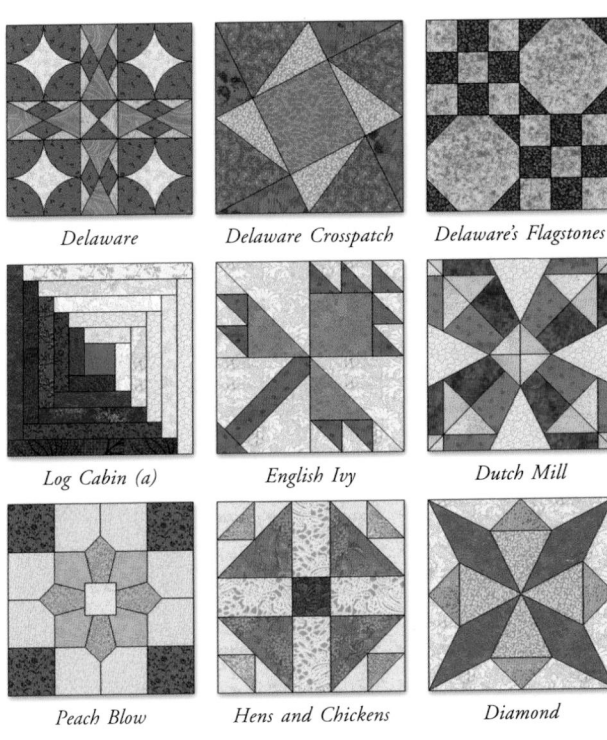

Delaware   Delaware Crosspatch   Delaware's Flagstones

Log Cabin (a)   English Ivy   Dutch Mill

Peach Blow   Hens and Chickens   Diamond

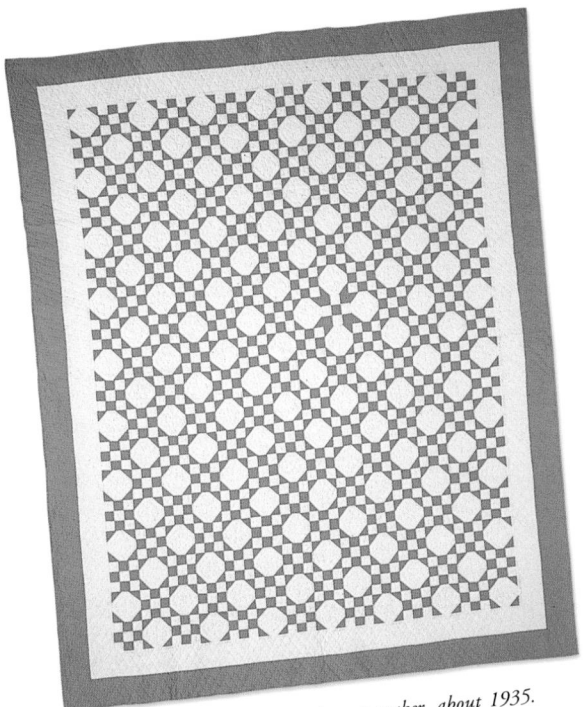

Delaware's Flagstones, unknown maker, about 1935. Delaware's Flagstones is one name for this two-block quilt, also called Snowball. Is the error in the pattern deliberate or an accident?

Delaware flip-flopped between English and Dutch rule throughout the seventeenth century. Remember the English with **English Ivy**, a 1931 *Kansas City Star* pattern. And think of the Dutch with a **Dutch Mill** block from the Ladies Art Company catalog.

Delaware has two nicknames, the First State and the Diamond State. To recall the latter, try the **Diamond** block, from a 1920 issue of *Farm News*.

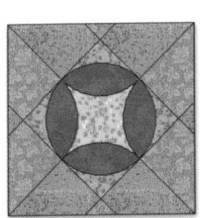

Dover

Eleven years after the Declaration of Independence from England, Delaware became the first of the United States when it ratified the new Constitution. Dover became the state capital. *Hearth and Home* magazine honored **Dover** with a block.

Remember the state flower, the Peach Blossom, with the **Peach Blow** block. The state bird is the Blue Hen chicken, so pick appropriate shades for a version of **Hen and Chickens** from Ruth Finley's 1929 book, *Old Patchwork Quilts and the Women Who Made Them.*

Peach Blossom

Holly

Blue Hen

State facts about...
Delaware

Date Entered Union:	**December 7, 1787**
Order of Admission:	**1**
State Capital:	**Dover**
State Flower:	**Peach blossom**
State Bird:	**Blue hen**
State Tree:	**Holly**
Nickname:	**First State, Diamond State**
Motto:	**Liberty and independence**

49

District of Columbia

In 1790, Congress authorized the building of a national capital, the District
of Columbia. The capital was later named Washington, for our first President.
During the nineteenth century, people called the capital Washington City,
but now many of us call it familiarly by its initials, just plain DC.

The quilter looking for Washington designs has a number to choose from. There are several patterns named for our first President and for the state of Washington. See the state of Washington on page 146 for more designs. The Ladies Art Company, which began selling mail-order quilt patterns in 1889, included a **Washington Sidewalk** block in their catalog. In the early 1930s, Ruby McKim gave a similar name, **Washington Pavement**, to the design more commonly known as Pineapple or Maltese Cross. **Washington's Puzzle**, also from the Ladies Art Company, and **Washington's Own**, from Carrie Hall's 1935 book, *The Romance of the Patchwork Quilt in America*, were probably named for George Washington.

Washington Sidewalk

"The Corcoran Gallery of Art, founded by William W. Corcoran in 1869, possesses valuable collections of paintings, sculptures and other works of art."

Washington's Puzzle   Washington Pavement   Washington's Own

Georgetown   Georgetown Circle (a)   Georgetown Circle (b)

Columbia   Washington Snowball   Rosebud

DC's flower, the American Beauty Rose, has long been a sentimental favorite.

Greetings from the nation's capital.

Washington's Own is sometimes called Potomac Pride, making it an excellent design for a District of Columbia quilt. Other names are Coronation or King's Crown, names that may have seemed a bit too royal for nineteenth-century Americans who admired Washington because he could have been king but chose to remain a commoner.

Hearth and Home magazine printed **Columbia** for South Carolina's capital, but the design can also stand for the District.

Georgetown, recalling the District of Columbia's historical neighborhood, appeared in the *Oklahoma Farmer* in 1896 and in the Ladies Art Company catalog as Georgetown Circle about the same time. Ruth Finley showed another **Georgetown Circle** (a) in her 1929 book, *Old Patchwork Quilts and the Women Who Made Them*. And Carrie Hall pictured a simpler **Georgetown Circle** (b) in her book.

Washington may be a Southern city, but a **Washington Snowball** is often possible. The District's flower is the American Beauty Rose. Although roses are usually appliquéd, you can piece a **Rosebud** from the Aunt Martha pattern company.

Rose

Scarlet Oak

Wood Thrush

Facts about...
District of Columbia

Date Established:	**December 1, 1800**
State Flower:	**American Beauty Rose**
State Bird:	**Wood thrush**
State Tree:	**Scarlet oak**
Nickname:	**Inside the Beltway**
Motto:	***Justitia omnibus***
	(Justice for all)

Florida
Sunshine State

Florida is known for its tropical scenery, citrus crops and the warm climate that makes it a Mecca for northern vacationers and retirees.

Like the other states, **Florida** was represented by a pattern in *Hearth and Home* magazine in the early twentieth century. Eveline Foland also featured the Orange Blossom State in her 1932 *Kansas City Star* column with a pattern for **Florida Star**. Remember the nickname, "The Sunshine State," with **Sunshine** (a) from the Ladies Art Company pattern catalog of the 1890s. Or try **Sunshine** (b) from Clara Stone's 1906 design.

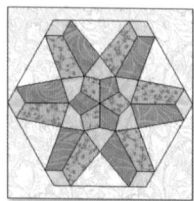

Florida Star

Tallahassee, Florida's capital city, was represented in the Ladies Art Company catalog. Key West, the tropical paradise known for its sunsets, at the southern tip of the state, was also included in that catalog as **Key West Beauty**. Key West so loves its tourists that in 1982 residents

Key West Beauty

protested a government roadblock by voting to secede from the union. They renamed the city the Conch Republic, joining the union again only after the roadblock was lifted.

Florida's indigenous tribes include the Seminole, a tribe well-known for intricate patchwork clothing. Remember them with the block,

Seminole Square, from *Chicago Tribune's* Nancy Cabot column in the 1930s. The first European settlers were the Spanish, who named the state "flower-filled," an accurate name that can be recalled with **Garden Walk**, a new name for an old pattern from the *Kansas City Star* in 1940.

Celebrate Florida's most famous crop with an **Orange Peel** (a) block from the Ladies Art Company, an **Orange Peel**(b) from 1930s designer, Ruby McKim, or yet another **Orange Peel**(c) from Carlie Sexton's pattern company of the 1930s. The state tree is the Palmetto. To stand for the tree use **Palm Leaf**, a popular pattern with early twentieth-century designers. The originator of the name, if not the design, was probably Ruby McKim.

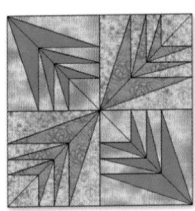
Palm Leaf

Florida   *Sunshine (a)*   *Sunshine (b)*

Tallahassee   *Seminole Square*   *Garden Walk*

Orange Peel (a)   *Orange Peel (b)*   *Orange Peel (c)*

State facts about...
Florida

Date Entered Union:	**March 3, 1845**
Order of Admission:	**27**
State Capital:	**Tallahassee**
State Flower:	**Orange blossom**
State Bird:	**Mockingbird**
State Tree:	**Palmetto**
Nickname:	**Orange State,**
	Sunshine State
Motto:	**In God we Trust**

Orange Blossom

Palmetto

Mockingbird

All the Way from Florida

199

321

PLACE ONE CENT STAMP HERE

MADE IN U.S.A.

This old postcard reads:
"The alligator is a native of the Florida Everglades. For some time its skin has been fashionably used in the manufacture of bags, shoes, etc., and with this increasing use they had been hunted until they were almost extinct. To remedy this situation and supply the demand, several thriving alligator farms are now in operation, where the breeding and care of alligators is the main industry."

Georgia
Peach State

Quilters with Georgia on their minds have named a few patterns
for their state and its history. The Creek and Cherokee Indian tribes settled
the land. The first European colonists arrived in 1733,
seeking refuge from religious persecution.

Savannah, their settlement, is honored with **Savannah Beautiful Star**, pictured in the Ladies Art Company's catalog of quilt patterns published in the early twentieth century.

Georgia

The colony was named for England's King George III. The block **Georgia** was sent to *Hearth and Home* magazine in the early twentieth century by a reader responding to its requests for patterns named for all the states. Twenty years later, *Workbasket* magazine modified the design and called it **State of Georgia** in their All-State Sampler Quilt.

Cotton became the chief crop after Eli Whitney's 1793 invention of the cotton gin in Georgia. His device for cleaning seeds from cotton was a technical milestone. It made growing, spinning, and weaving

127— SCENE ON THE BEAUTIFUL CHATTAHOOCHEE RIVER, ATLANTA, GA.

The Chattahoochee River near Atlanta.

cotton practical and economical, resulting in the classic American patchwork quilt. **The Cotton Boll Quilt** block will recall King Cotton and its effect on the history of both the state and quiltmaking. The pattern appeared in a 1941 *Kansas City Star*.

Marietta Blockhouse

Marietta Blockhouse is a pattern from the *Chicago Tribune's* Nancy Cabot column. This column was affiliated with the *Progressive Farmer* quilt pattern syndicate. Since the *Progressive Farmer* was a southern agricultural magazine, it explains why so many southern designs were printed in the *Chicago Tribune*. This particular block may have something to do with Marietta, Georgia, which has been characterized as Georgia's gayest, most fashionable town in the decade before the Civil War.

Atlanta, a railroad center, soon overtook Marietta as the state's primary city. A *Hearth and Home* reader honored **Atlanta** when the magazine asked for patterns named for the state capitals. This design requires two blocks set alternately like an Irish Chain.

Macon's Washington Park.

The state Capitol Building in the 1950's.

Georgia's Civil War role is remembered with many memorials. **Confederate Rose**, a pieced design from the Cabot column, is one of the few Confederate patterns in print. But it's doubtful that this design was made during the Civil War. **Sherman's March**, another Civil War name that has come down to us, recalls the Union Army's devastation of Georgia and the burning of Atlanta.

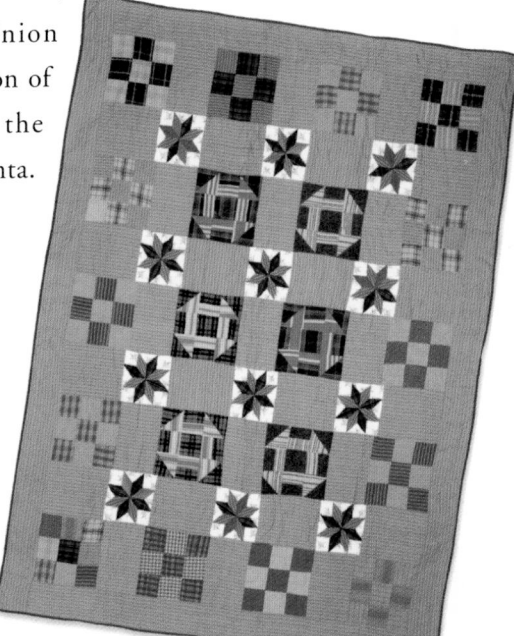

Sherman's March by Terry Clothier Thompson, Lawrence, Kansas, 1996. Terry wanted the look of an old Southern linsey quilt, so she used cotton flannel.

Savannah Beautiful Star State of Georgia The Cotton Boll Quilt

Atlanta Confederate Rose Sherman's March

Peach Blow Live Oak Tree Birds in the Air

No. 4291 N. The "Cherokee Rose" Quilt

Gingham patches in deep pink, yellow and green are used for the roses.
The bands are of light pink, both across quilt and around border

Georgia's state flower is the Cherokee Rose. Marie Webster designed a Cherokee Rose quilt for Needlecraft Magazine in 1930. The blocks were adapted from a traditional design. The "quaint little potted trees" in the border were Webster's own.

It was first published in a *Capper's Weekly/Famous Features* pattern booklet in the mid-twentieth century. You are probably more familiar with one of the design's thirty or so other names, including Shoo Fly and Churn Dash.

Georgia has several nicknames. The best known is "The Peach State," which can be symbolized with **Peach Blow** from Clara Stone's 1906 booklet of quilt patterns. A "blow," according to my dictionary, is an archaic or poetic word for blossom.

Cracker

Another Georgia nickname is "The Cracker State," represented with the design known as **Cracker** published in *Woman's World* magazine around 1930. The state tree is the **Live Oak Tree**, a pattern included in an early edition of the Ladies Art Company catalog around 1890. The

state bird is the Brown Thrasher. **Birds In The Air**, a pieced design from Ruth Finley's 1929 book, *Old Patchwork Quilts and the Women Who Made Them*, would do nicely if the birds (the triangles) were shades of brown.

Cherokee Rose

Live Oak

Brown Thrasher

State facts about...
Georgia

Date Entered Union:	**January 2, 1788**
Order of Admission:	**4**
State Capital:	**Atlanta**
State Flower:	**Cherokee rose**
State Bird:	**Brown thrasher**
State Tree:	**Live oak**
Nickname:	**Peach State**
Motto:	**Wisdom, justice, and moderation**

Hawaii

Aloha State

Quilters know Hawaii best through the tradition
of Hawaiian quilts made with intricately folded and cut patterns
representing island foliage and scenery.

Hawaii has also inspired mainland pattern designers over the years, resulting in quilt blocks named for the state and its beauties. **Hawaii** was printed in *Hearth and Home* magazine about 1910.

Hawaii

The magazine encouraged readers to send designs named for states and U.S. possessions. A few years later they printed **Honolulu** for the capital city.

Polynesian people who sailed north across the Pacific settled the islands centuries ago. Remember their voyage with **Ocean Wave**, a popular pattern at the end of last century. Ruby McKim showed it as a square block in her 1931 book, *101 Patchwork Patterns*.

But the block can also be a six-sided pieced unit and a plain square. European settlers renamed the islands the Sandwich Islands in the 1770s, but the Polynesian name was maintained when Hawaii became a U.S. possession in 1898.

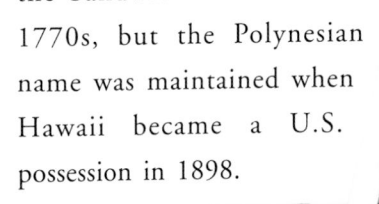

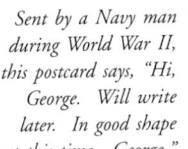

Sent by a Navy man during World War II, this postcard says, "Hi, George. Will write later. In good shape at this time. George."

Hawaii

by Pamela Mayfield, Lawrence, Kansas, 2000.
Machine-appliquéd and machine-quilted. Pamela adapted a Hawaiian appliqué center
"Coconut and Pineapple," (not on CD) rather than using pieced blocks.
Her border combines hibiscus blossoms with kukui leaves.

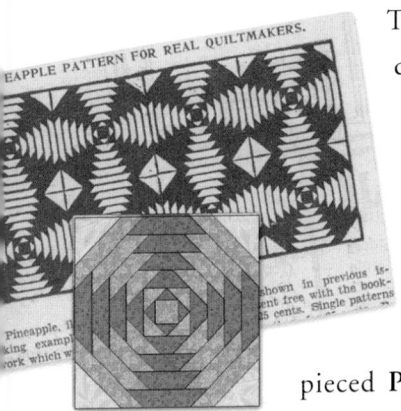

The European colonists developed a sugar industry, which can be recalled with **Sugar Bowl**, a *Farm Journal* design. Pineapples are also an important Hawaiian crop. The pieced **Pineapple** pattern has been a favorite design since the 1880s. Carrie Hall recorded the name in her 1935 book, *The Romance of the Patchwork Quilt in America*.

Pineapple

In 1959, Hawaii became the 50th star on the U.S. flag. Use a **Star of the West** to symbolize the westernmost state. Ruth Finley recorded the pattern name in her 1929 book, *Old Patchwork Quilts and the Women Who Made Them*. This old design was originally named for Henry Clay, a politician from Kentucky, when that state was considered the West. In the early part of the nineteenth century few Americans could imagine there would once be a state as distant as Hawaii.

Star of the West

Today's air travel makes tourism one of Hawaii's biggest industries. Travelers come to enjoy the scenery as they lie in the tropical sun. **The Tropical Sun**

Honolulu *Ocean Wave* *Sugar Bowl*

The Tropical Sun *Diamond Head* *Goose Tracks*

block – a variation of a block known as Mariner's Compass – is from the Home Art Company, a 1930s pattern house. Symbolize Hawaii's natural beauty with **Diamond Head**, an Oahu landmark and a pattern that appeared in the *Chicago Tribune's* Nancy Cabot column in 1936.

The state bird is the nene, the Hawaiian goose, who can leave his mark with **Goose Tracks** from the Ladies Art Company's 1889 pattern catalog.

"World famous Waikiki Beach and Diamond Head"

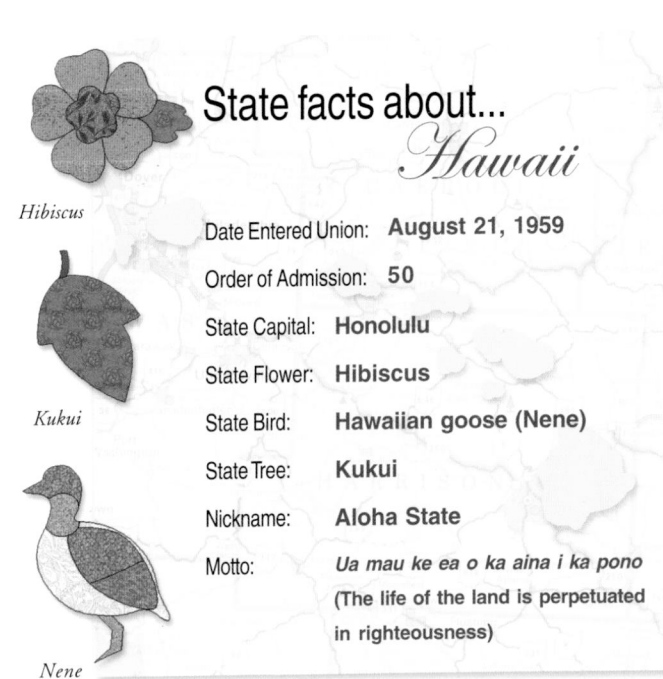

Hibiscus

Kukui

Nene

State facts about...
Hawaii

Date Entered Union:	**August 21, 1959**
Order of Admission:	**50**
State Capital:	**Honolulu**
State Flower:	**Hibiscus**
State Bird:	**Hawaiian goose (Nene)**
State Tree:	**Kukui**
Nickname:	**Aloha State**
Motto:	*Ua mau ke ea o ka aina i ka pono* (The life of the land is perpetuated in righteousness)

Idaho

Idaho became the 43rd state on July 3, 1890. The origins of its name
are unclear. The senators naming the Idaho Territory (formed in 1863) believed
Idaho was an Indian word for "Gem of the Mountains."
But they were misinformed.

*S*ome trace "Eee-dah-how" to a greeting in Shoshone. Whatever its meaning, the anglicized word sounded lofty and impressive to senatorial ears, so they applied it to the mountainous territory where gold had recently been discovered.

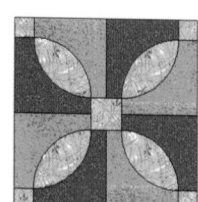

Idaho (a)

Idaho (a) is the pattern that *Hearth and Home* magazine published in its early- twentieth-century state design series. Twenty years later, *Workbasket* magazine published another **Idaho** (b) (also called The Gem Block), particularly appropriate for the state nicknamed "The Gem State."

Idaho Beauty was published in Clara Stone's 1906 catalog, *Practical Needlework*. In 1965, Lela B. Williams designed **Idaho Star**, inspired by Sun Valley ski trails, for the state pattern series in *Aunt*

Karl Liermauer and Family, Buhl, Idaho, about 1910.

60

Idaho (b) Idaho Beauty Idaho Star

Boise Farm Friendliness Pine Tree

canyon (deeper than the Grand Canyon) can be remembered with **Snake Trail**, published in the book *Kentucky Quilts and Their Makers*. (This double fan pattern is also known as Railroad Around Rocky Mountain.)

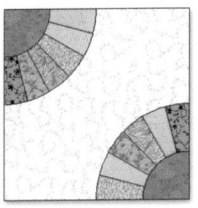

Snake Trail

Kate's Quilting Bee magazine. **Boise** was named for the state capital in *Hearth and Home's* capital city series in 1916.

Idaho's chief crop is its famous potatoes. **Farm Friendliness**, from *Farm Journal* magazine, can represent the state's agriculture. Idaho's natural beauties, such as Hell's Canyon on the Snake River, are also important to its economy. The river and its

Another of Idaho's natural wonders, the Sawtooth Mountains, is represented by **Sawtooth** from Carrie Hall's 1935 index to quilt patterns, *The Romance of the Patchwork Quilt in America*.

Sawtooth

The state tree is the western white pine, or mountain pine. From the many pieced pine tree designs, I chose **Pine Tree**, published in the *Farmer's Wife* magazine in 1931.

Vacationing teacher, Miss Mitchell, sent a postcard of Twin Falls to her student, Zoe, in 1914.

Syringa

Western White Pine Cone

Mountain Bluebird

State facts about...
Idaho

Date Entered Union:	**July 3, 1890**
Order of Admission:	**43**
State Capital:	**Boise**
State Flower:	**Syringa**
State Bird:	**Mountain bluebird**
State Tree:	**Western white pine**
Nickname:	**Gem of the Mountains**
Motto:	***Esto perpetua* (It is forever)**

Illinois
Land of Lincoln

Why are so many designs named for Illinois places and history?
Credit has to go to the Nancy Cabot column in the *Chicago Tribune*,
which printed daily patterns throughout the 1930s.

Nancy (her real name was Loretta Leitner Rising) designed many original patterns, and named them for the local landscape. Another

"Hello, how art thou. How are the folks? Did not get to see you Sunday. Picked 1 gallon of berries this morning."

important event that inspired Illinois patterns was the 1933 Century of Progress in Quiltmaking contest, held at the World's Fair in Chicago. That fair celebrated Chicago's

Illinois

centennial as a city. Nearly 25,000 quilters entered the quilt contest, adding to the state's image as a center for quiltmaking.

Illinois was named for the large Indian tribe called the Illini or Illiniwek, which meant "the people." When European explorers first entered the region in the seventeenth century, there were about 10,000

Chicago Pavements

Illinois Star (a)

Illinois Star (b)

Lincoln's Platform (a)

Lincoln's Platform (b)

Nauvoo Lattice

Going to Chicago

World's Fair

Arrant Red Birds

Chicago Skyline: Less is More and Easier to Appliqué, by Barbara Brackman, Chicago, Illinois, 1977. I used the Chicago Star for the set.

A patriotic quartet about 1890 in Macomb, Illinois.

Illiniwek, including smaller groups such as the Michigamea, the Peoria and the Cahokia. By 1885, war, disease, and western expansion had reduced their number to about 150. Descendants of the Illiniwek, who were relocated to Indian Territory, now live in Oklahoma.

The French were the first non-native people to control the region. They left few lasting marks, except for the spelling of place names. Illiniwek, became Illinois, a subtle change if one pronounces the word as the French would: Il'-in-wah. Americans took over the territory after the Revolution, and in 1818 Illinois became a state.

The state's early history can be remembered with a variety of Illinois patterns. **Illinois** is from *Hearth and Home* magazine's series of state patterns. **Illinois Star** (a) is from

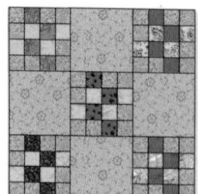

Illinois Road

Workbasket magazine's series. Another **Illinois Star** (b) was designed by Betty Flack of Shumway, Illinois, for a 1964 issue of *Aunt Kate's Quilting Bee*, a small magazine for pattern collectors. The star is formed from ears of corn, a major state crop. In 1935, Nancy Cabot printed a pattern called **Illinois Road**.

Lincoln's Cabin Home

Illinois is "The Land of Lincoln." Naturally there are several patterns honoring the Illinois lawyer who saved the Union. **Lincoln's Cabin Home**, from *Hearth and Home* magazine, recalls Lincoln's pioneer origins. **The Lincoln Quilt** was named by needlework designer Anne Orr,

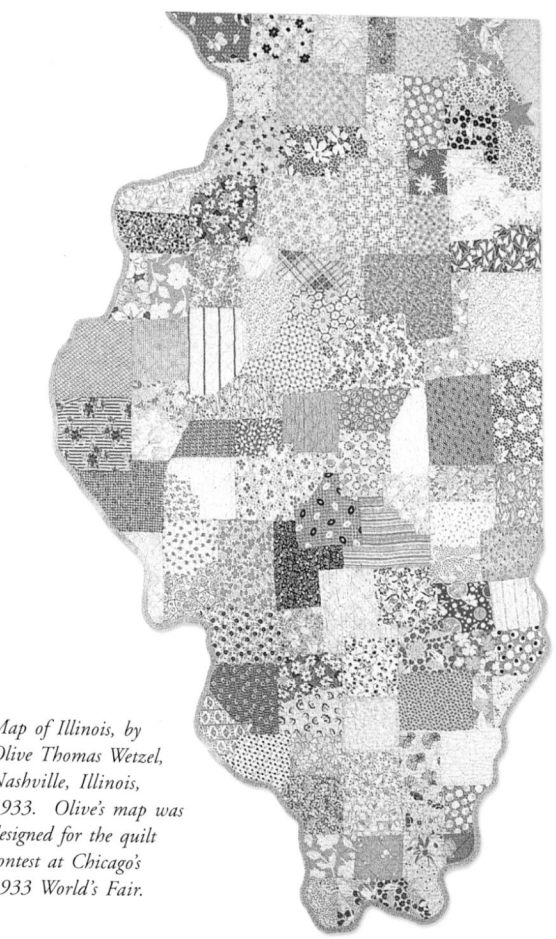

Map of Illinois, by Olive Thomas Wetzel, Nashville, Illinois, 1933. Olive's map was designed for the quilt contest at Chicago's 1933 World's Fair.

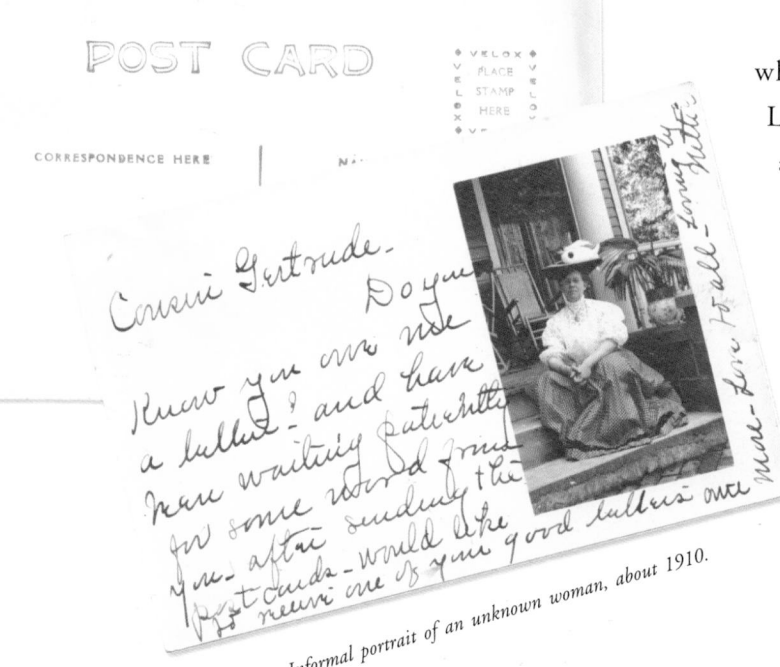

Informal portrait of an unknown woman, about 1910.

who wrote that Abraham Lincoln's mother had made a quilt in that design before his birth. The story may be a myth, but the combination of

The Lincoln Quilt

stars and checkerboards makes a beautiful quilt. **Lincoln's Platform** is represented in two patterns: one (a) named by Carrie Hall in her 1935 book *The Romance of the Patchwork Quilt in America*, and the other (b) from Ladies Art Company's late-nineteenth-century catalog.

Springfield

Many Illinois cities have their own patterns. **Springfield**, the state capital, was honored with a block in *Hearth and Home*. Chicago, the state's biggest city, has several patterns.

Chicago Pavements is from Clara Stone who published a *Pratical Needlework: Quilt Patterns* booklet in 1906. **Chicago Star** is from the Ladies Art Company. **Going to Chicago**, a new name for an old design honoring the World's Fair that year, appeared in the syndicated *Nancy Page* column in 1933. A **World's Fair** block (subtitled Chicago Century of Progress) is from the Laura Wheeler/Alice Brooks syndicate. Smaller

Chicago Star

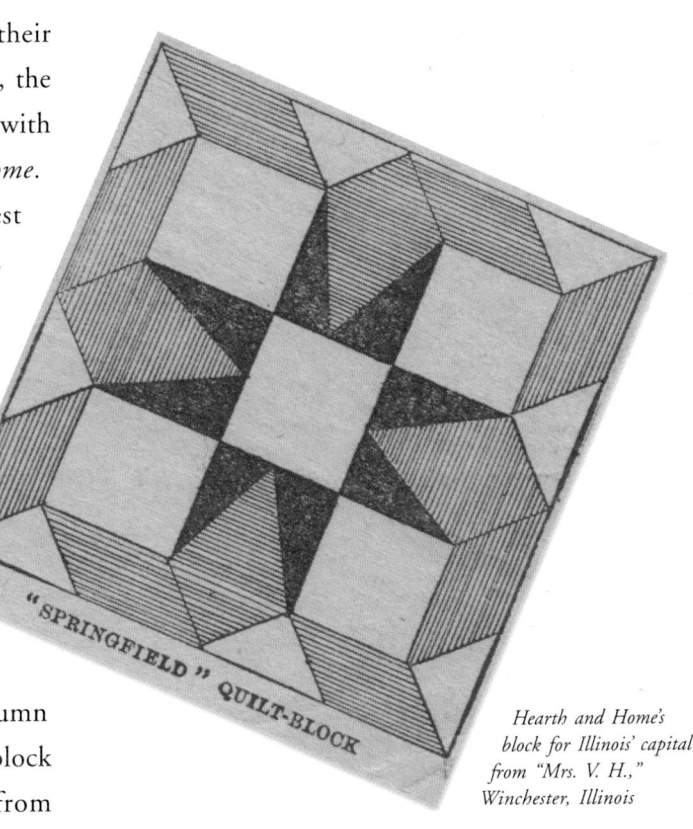

"SPRINGFIELD" QUILT-BLOCK

Hearth and Home's block for Illinois' capital from "Mrs. V. H.," Winchester, Illinois

State facts about...
Illinois

Date Entered Union:	**December 3, 1818**
Order of Admission:	**21**
State Capital:	**Springfield**
State Flower:	**Violet**
State Bird:	**Cardinal**
State Tree:	**White oak**
Nickname:	**Land of Lincoln**
Motto:	**State sovereignty, national union**

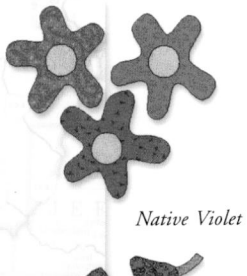

Native Violet

White Oak

Cardinal

Illinois settlements were also remembered in the Nancy Cabot newspaper pattern column. **Bishop Hill** was a Swedish community. **Nauvoo Lattice** recalls a Mormon town.

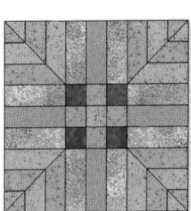

Bishop Hill

The state tree is the native oak, long a favorite pattern inspiration for quiltmakers. The Illinois State Register printed a traditional version of **The Oak Leaf** in 1932. Nancy Cabot gave us a pieced pattern for the state bird, the Cardinal, in **Arrant Red Birds**, published in 1936.

The Oak Leaf

Indiana

Hoosier State

Indiana's melodious name came from a commercial company
of land speculators. They claimed a large tract on the banks of the Ohio River,
calling themselves "The Indiana Company" by latinizing
Columbus' name for the native Americans.

By the time Congress established the Indiana Territory, Hoosiers were using that name for part of what was once called the Northwest Territories.

We can remember those early settlers with **Indiana Farmer**, a Nancy Cabot design from the *Chicago Tribune*. Remember the state's native tribes, and those pushed west from there,

Indiana Farmer

with another Nancy Cabot block, **Woodland Path**. **Indiana** is *Hearth and Home* magazine's contribution to Indiana quilt lore.

Indiana Puzzle is a popular name for intricate designs, an indication of Indiana quilters' reputation. One **Indiana Puzzle** (a) pattern is from pattern designer Carlie Sexton in 1930. Another **Indiana Puzzle** (b) is a *Kansas City Star* design from the same year. Mae Wilford, a 1930s Chicago designer, called her design

Grassyfork Fisheries claimed they were the "World's Largest Fisheries-Water Gardens Nurseries." Ethel's note just mentioned the heat.

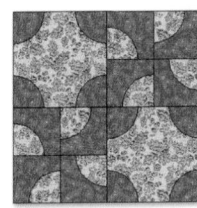

Indiana Pumpkin Vine

(a variation of the Drunkard's Path), Indiana Puzzle or **Indiana Pumpkin Vine**. Ruby McKim's **Indiana Puzzle** (c) is from her *Patchwork Parade of States* in the early 1930s. And in 1976, *Quilter's Newsletter Magazine* gave the name **Indiana Puzzle** (d) to a block also known as Snail's Trail and Monkey Wrench.

Indianapolis

Indianapolis, the state capital, is represented by a reader contribution from *Hearth and Home* magazine. **Harrison Rose**, from the *Rural New Yorker* in 1930, remembers President William Henry Harrison, one of Indiana's favorite sons, who governed the Northwest Territory and ran for President as "Old Tippecanoe." He died within a month of his inauguration. **Old Tippecanoe**, from the Ladies Art Company, remembers his campaign.

Woodland Path — *Indiana* — *Indiana Puzzle (a)*

Indiana Puzzle (b) — *Indiana Puzzle (c)* — *Indiana Puzzle (d)*

Harrison Rose — *Old Tippecanoe* — *The Peony*

Indiana's state flower is the peony. Ruth Finley pictured a traditional nineteenth-century block, **The Peony**, in her 1929 book, *Old Patchwork Quilts and the Women Who Made Them*. The Laura Wheeler syndicated column designed three pieced **Peonies** (a,b,c) in the 1930s.

State facts about...
Indiana

Date Entered Union:	December 11, 1816
Order of Admission:	19
State Capital:	**Indianapolis**
State Flower:	**Peony**
State Bird:	**Cardinal**
State Tree:	**Tulip tree**
Nickname:	**Hoosier State**
Motto:	**Crossroads of America**

Peony

Tulip Tree

Cardinal

The word "peony" may be derived from the Greek word for Apollo, a god associated with beauty and the sun.

Indiana State Flower

Peony (a) — *Peony (b)* — *Peony (c)*

Iowa
Hawkeye State

The word Iowa comes from the French interpretation
of Indian names.

Explorers Louis Jolliet and (Father) Jacques Marquette recorded the names of tribes living in the region. On the river they named for the Messouri they heard of the Maha and Ouaouiatonon people. They added O to the Maha for the people on the west bank. And they subtracted syllables from Ouaouiatonon, making the Ouaouia, the Ayoua, the Ioway and eventually the Iowa.

The **Iowa** block was sent by a reader to *Hearth and Home* magazine about 1910, when the editor was looking for a pattern for every state. About the same time, the Ladies Art Company began offering a pattern they called **Iowa Star**.

Iowan Carlie Sexton was well-known as a writer on the topic of antique quilts during the 1920s and 1930s. Born in Pella, Iowa, she spent much of her life in Des Moines, writing for such Iowa publications as *Wallace's Farmer* and *Better Homes and Gardens*. She also had a mail-order pattern company.

Unknown child, about 1870, photographed in Waverly, Iowa.

68

Another Iowa pattern company was Home Art Studios, run by H. H. Ver Mehren in Des Moines in the 1930s. **Des Moines** is Iowa's state capitol, celebrated by a block sent to *Hearth and Home* magazine around 1910. The city has long been a major crossroads for travel in the upper midwest. Remember the town and Ver Mehren's quilt pattern company with **Cross Roads**.

The state tree is the oak. **Oak Leaf** was published in the Illinois State Register in 1932. Iowa is a major farming state, represented by **Corn and Beans** and **Country Farm**, both from the Ladies Art Company. **Prairie Sunrise**, from *Hearth and Home*, can represent northern Iowa's landscape, among the continent's broadest and flattest prairies. **Hill and Hollow**, from Nancy Cabot in 1937, stands for the southern valleys and the bluffs along the Mississippi River.

Iowa *Iowa Star* *Des Moines*

Oak Leaf *Cross Roads* *Corn and Beans*

Country Farm *Prairie Sunrise* *Hill and Hollow*

Ruby Short McKim's quilt patterns were syndicated to a number of newspapers from the teens through the 1930s.

State facts about...
Iowa

Date Entered Union:	December 28, 1846
Order of Admission:	29
State Capital:	Des Moines
State Flower:	Wild rose
State Bird:	Eastern goldfinch
State Tree:	White/red oak
Nickname:	Hawkeye State
Motto:	Our liberties we prize, our rights we will maintain

Wild Rose

White/Red Oak

Eastern Goldfinch

'Corn and Beans' Pattern Was Favorite With Our Grandmothers

It's the Sixth Block In Old Patchwork Quilt.

Corn and Beans, by Georgann Eglinski, Lawrence, Kansas, 1999. Quilted by Shirley Greenhoe. Georgann used a field of Corn and Beans around the Laurel Leaves appliqué.

Kansas

by Jean Stanclift, Lawrence, Kansas, 2001.
Machine-appliquéd by Jean Stanclift. Machine-quilted by Pamela Mayfield.
Kansas Trouble blocks are bordered by a vine of sunflowers, meadowlark and cottonwood leaves.

Kansas

Sunflower State

Kansas, in the center of the continental United States, has a reputation
for being in the middle of any quiltmaking activity. During times when the craft was
unfashionable in urban areas, Kansans kept up their quilting tradition.
And during quilt revivals, they quilt with the best of them.

Two stars of the 1930s' quilt revival were Kansans: Emporia neighbors Charlotte Jane Whitehill and Rose Kretsinger. Both now have quilts hanging in the Denver Art Museum and the Spencer Museum of Art in Lawrence, Kansas.

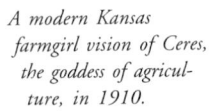

A modern Kansas farmgirl vision of Ceres, the goddess of agriculture, in 1910.

Leavenworth, Kansas was home to quilt historian Carrie Hall, remembered for her 1935 quilt pattern index, *The Romance of the Patchwork Quilt in America*, picturing many designs named for her home state. Less well-known are the Kansas Amish and Mennonite quilters whose striking work appears in many books.

Kansas

Kansas does seem to have more patterns named for it than any other state. This is probably due less to its excellent quilters and more to some strategically placed pattern companies and periodicals. The central plains were the center for pattern sales and publication in the mid-twentieth century, with most of the important sources located between El Dorado, Kansas, and Chicago.

Some companies solicited patterns from local quiltmakers who were glad to send in favorite designs, many named for their state. Few patterns seem to have been named for Kansas in the nineteenth-century. Most were named later by commercial pattern companies and newspaper columnists. **Rocky Road to Kansas** (a) was a string quilt design popular around the country after 1880. Immigrants who settled after 1854 may have named the design. But the name Rocky Road to Kansas first appeared with the pattern about 1890 in the Ladies Art Company catalog.

Kansas Troubles reflects problems the early settlers brought with them. Northerners and Southerners scrambled to control territorial government, and guerilla warfare scourged Kansas for years before the Civil War was formally declared. The quilt pattern appeared in quilts made during the years when the territory was known as "Bleeding Kansas." But what the quiltmakers called those quilts is unknown. The

Rocky Road to Kansas (a) *Rocky Road to Kansas (b)* *Kansas Troubles*

Kansas Sunflower (a) *Kansas Sunflower (b)* *Kansas Dugout*

The Kansas Dust Storm *Kansas Star* *Topeka*

name Kansas Troubles wasn't recorded until the Ladies Art Company published it thirty years later. In her 1929 book, *Old Patchwork Quilts and The Women Who Made Them*, Ruth Finley included the pattern, also known as **Rocky Road to Kansas** (b). The road remained rocky after the Civil War, when nature could be as threatening as the earlier border wars. Many young families, immigrating to Kansas looking for free land and a new life away from the war-scarred East, had to survive blizzards, drought, and grasshopper plagues by living in a hole in the ground. Since there were no forests to provide lumber for houses, most newcomers began their Kansas years in a dugout. These homes, sod-covered shelters dug into the ground or hillside, were nostalgically recalled in the block called **Kansas Dugout** from Aunt Martha.

A postcard from the 1940s featuring views and symbols of the Sunflower State.

Kansas farmers show off the stove and the cow in front of a sod house.

A BASKET of KANSAS PEACHES

The 1908 message to Dena Thompson on the reverse of this card is rather wistful. "Am gone again. Am at Hutchinson. Suppose I will stay here all winter. Lester. General Delivery."

Kansas map, by Harriet Angelia Deuel, Wyandotte County, Kansas, 1887. Collection of the Kansas Museum of History. Oklahoma was still Indian Territory when Harriet Deuel stitched her map of Kansas. Photo courtesy of the Kansas Quilt Project.

Kansas may not have had many trees, but it had grassy, rolling plains covered with sunflowers. This state flower is commemorated in many patterns. The *Household* magazine, published in Topeka, printed a **Kansas Sunflower** (a) in 1915. Carrie Hall included a simpler version (b) in her 1935 book.

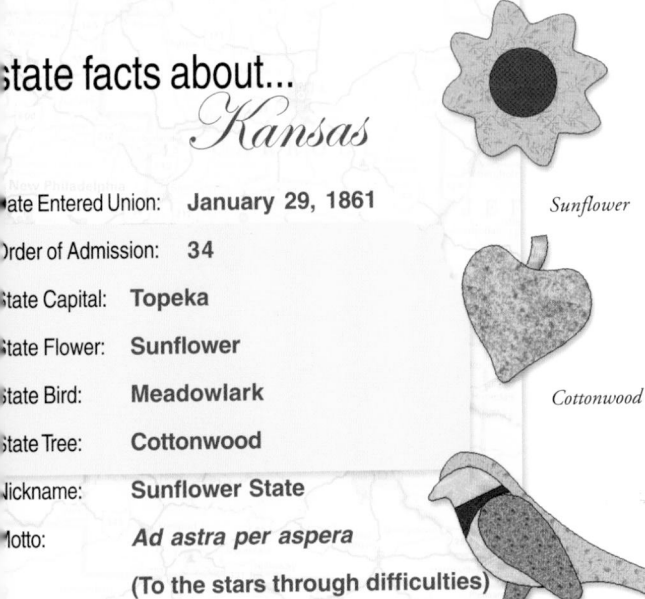

state facts about...
Kansas

State Entered Union:	**January 29, 1861**
Order of Admission:	**34**
State Capital:	**Topeka**
State Flower:	**Sunflower**
State Bird:	**Meadowlark**
State Tree:	**Cottonwood**
Nickname:	**Sunflower State**
Motto:	***Ad astra per aspera***
	(To the stars through difficulties)

Sunflower

Cottonwood

Meadowlark

Settlers who learned to live and farm in the extreme Kansas climate grew to love their state's beauty. Their descendants take great pride in its agricultural abundance; the state produces more wheat than any other. The beauty of Kansas is remembered in **Kansas Beauty**, which was sent to the *Kansas City Star* in 1936 by Roberta Christy of

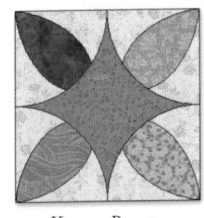

Kansas Beauty

Scott City. By then, times were again as tough as they'd been in the 1870s, a fact commemorated by another reader of the *Star's* pattern column who sent **The Kansas Dust Storm** in 1935. The *Kansas City Star* printed many Kansas patterns, among them **Kansas Star**, designed in 1932 by their illustrator, Eveline Foland.

Hearth and Home magazine, an earlier publication, also asked readers to send in their favorite designs. They named one pattern **Kansas**, and honored **Topeka**, the state capital, with another block.

Kentucky
Bluegrass State

In the 1920s and 1930s, during the glory years of the quilt pattern industry, when hundreds of newspapers carried some kind of quilt column, Kentucky was known as *the* place for quiltmaking.

Several cottage industries that sold finished quilts advertised their goods were "handmade by the women of Kentucky," no matter where the business was located (according to quilt historian Cuesta Benberry.) Two competing quilt retailers, the Eleanor Beard Studio and the Nancy Lincoln Guild, faced each other on New York City's Madison Avenue. Both pointed out that their exquisite quilts were sewn by Kentucky quilters.

Unknown woman photographed in Louisville about 1865.

The Kentucky quilter's celebrity is one reason we find so many Kentucky patterns in the press. Pieced designs named for the state include **State of Kentucky** sent by Mrs. L.W. to *Hearth and Home* magazine when the editors requested a block for each state about 1916. Mrs. L.W. was from Mt. Vernon, Indiana, but she had copied an old quilt made by her Kentucky grandmother, "and we always called it 'the Kentucky quilt' so I think it may well represent that state," she wrote.

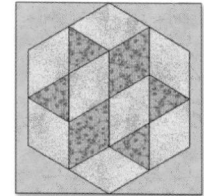

State of Kentucky

Needlecraft magazine published **Old Kentucky Home**, sent by Sister May of Allegheny, Pennsylvania. Although quilters today consider this design a schoolhouse, it was often viewed as a log cabin in the early twentieth century. An unusual log cabin version was published in *Capper's Weekly* in 1934 as **Abe Lincoln's Log Cabin**, named for the president born in a Kentucky cabin.

Kentucky Crossroads first appeared in the *Prairie Farmer* in 1930. About that time, Lockport Batting Company published **Kentucky Quilt**, a complex Feathered Star. Carrie Hall in her 1935 index to quilt patterns gave the name **Kentucky Beauty** to a pattern also known as Strawberry, among other names. Not one of these publications originated in Kentucky. But the names show the mystique Kentucky quilts held for decades.

The height of Kentucky's acclaim came in 1933, when a Lexington woman, Margaret Rodgers Caden, won the top award in one of the largest quilt contests ever held. Nearly 25,000 quilters from across America entered the competition, sponsored by Sears, Roebuck and Company at the Chicago World's Fair. Of 30 finalists, six were from Kentucky. Winner Caden took home a $1,000 prize (the price of a luxury car in those days) with her Star of the Bluegrass, a pattern still in print from Mountain Mist.

Star of the Bluegrass, unknown makers, Kentucky, about 1934. Collection of the Caden Family. Margaret Caden asked her Kentucky quiltmakers to make a second version of the quilt that won the 1933 Chicago World's Fair.

But did Caden really make the quilt? My fellow quilt researcher, Merikay Waldvogel, and I did some detective work. We discovered that Margaret Caden actually did not put a single stitch into her prizewinning quilt! The quilt was, like many others sold in her Caden's needlework and gift shop, a product of local cottage industries. The Star of the

Old Kentucky Home

Abe Lincoln's Log Cabin

Kentucky Crossroads

Kentucky Quilt

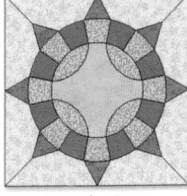
Kentucky Beauty

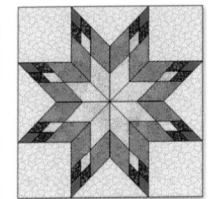
Kentucky's Twinkling Star

Bluegrass was a group project pieced by Ida Rhorer, stuffed by Mattie Black and quilted by Allie Price and her daughters. Caden's deception is shocking in light of our contemporary attitudes about originality, but the scandal takes nothing away from the skills of the Kentucky quiltmakers. Had Ida, Mattie, and Allie received the credit due them, Kentucky still would have been tops in quiltmaking in the 1930s.

The pattern's popularity has endured. In 1979, *Good Housekeeping* sponsored a national contest and a variation, **Kentucky's Twinkling Star**, was a state winner.

State facts about...
Kentucky

Goldenrod

Coffee Tree

Cardinal

Date Entered Union:	**June 1, 1792**
Order of Admission:	**15**
State Capital:	**Frankfort**
State Flower:	**Goldenrod**
State Bird:	**Cardinal**
State Tree:	**Coffee tree**
Nickname:	**Bluegrass State**
Motto:	**United we stand,**
	Divided we fall

Louisiana
Bayou State

Mardi Gras is America's biggest carnival. Put yourself
in a Mardi Gras mood any time of year with a trip to Louisiana
through quilt patterns.

The **Louisiana** pattern was named for the state by a Shreveport reader of *Hearth and Home* magazine who responded to the 1907 request for blocks representing the states and their capitals. Later

Baton Rouge

"Louisiana Lou" sent **Baton Rouge** for the capital city. In the 1930s, Nancy Cabot, the quilt columnist for the *Chicago Tribune* and other newspapers around the country, printed **Baton Rouge Square**.

Louisiana was settled by the French, who named it for their king. Ruth Finley, in her 1929 book, *Old Patchwork Quilts and the Women Who Made Them*, tells of the founding of New Orleans, by Jean- Baptiste Le Moyne, the Sieur de Bienville, and how the eight pointed diamond star came to be named for him. The Star of LeMoyne or **LeMoyne Star** (a), a design found

in needlework long before anyone imagined a Louisiana, now symbolizes New Orleans to quiltmakers. Margaret Ickis showed a variation called **LeMoyne Star** (b) in her 1949 book, *The Standard Book of Quiltmaking*. (In 1956, Lela Williams showed the same pattern in the magazine *Aunt Kate's Quilting Bee* and called it Louisiana Star. To make piecing easier, she suggested using a wide striped fabric and placing the diamonds' points right on the stripe, since eight seams meeting in the center lie flatter than 16.)

State handkerchiefs, with maps and state flowers, were perfect souveniers for travelers to collect.

76

French Star

Nancy Cabot showed a **French Star** describing it as a pattern "brought to New Orleans by French settlers in the earliest days of Louisiana's history." Since there is no evidence of any pieced quilts on this continent in those very early days, we can take Nancy's story as an exaggeration. But the pattern is a nice way to remember France's contribution to much of Louisiana's language and customs. Their descendants are known as Creoles, and **Creole Puzzle** is another Nancy Cabot pattern.

Magnolia Bud

Louisiana became a state in 1812, after Thomas Jefferson purchased the territory from the French. Today, its official state bird is the brown pelican and its tree is the cypress. The state flower, the magnolia, has several quilt block designs. Eveline Foland, who drew patterns for the *Kansas City Star*, designed **Magnolia Bud** in 1932. **Magnolia**

Louisiana   *Baton Rouge Square*   *Creole Puzzle*

LeMoyne Star (a)   *LeMoyne Star (b)*   *Magnolia*

Carnival Time   *Carnival*   *Mardi Gras*

is a design from the Laura Wheeler syndicated column around the same time. The Laura Wheeler column also featured **Mardi Gras**. With a scrapbag full of colorful prints, it would be a festive quilt, as would **Carnival Time** from the Aunt Martha Studios, or **Carnival** from Nancy Cabot.

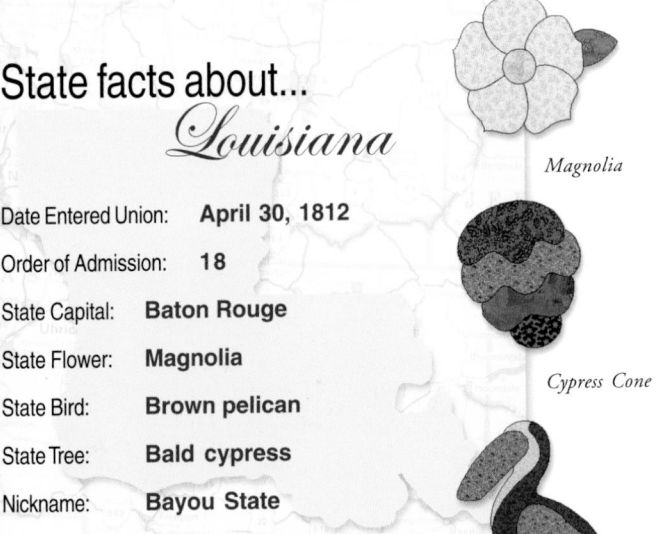

Magnolia

Cypress Cone

Brown Pelican

Louisiana Rose by Celia Pardue Hyde, Crowley, Louisiana, 1930-1933. Collection of Marjorie Malone. Celia Hyde's original design in cotton sateen won several prizes at the 1933 Chicago World's Fair's quilt contest.

Maine

Pine Tree State

The Maine landscape, with its coasts and forests, inspires many pictorial quilt artists. Those who want to recall Maine more abstractly can stitch up patterns named for the state and its features.

For nearly two centuries, colonial Maine was nothing more than northern Massachusetts. But in 1820, Maine became a state in its own right.

Maine

About 90 years later, the pattern **Maine** appeared in *Hearth and Home* magazine's series of state designs, sent in by an anonymous reader who called herself "A Daughter of Maine." The magazine also named a block for every state capital, so **Augusta** has its own block.

Maine is the largest New England state, a geographical fact you can mark with the pattern **New England Block**. Maine also has more forestland (84 percent) than any other state, the reason for its nickname. In the 1930s, the widely syndicated Nancy Page quilt pattern column printed **Maine Woods**. The corner triangles represent the pine trees and underbrush.

"Augusta" from Hearth and Home magazine.

78

GREETINGS FROM DANFORTH, MAINE

"Mother" sent this postcard from Danforth, Maine, in June, 1950. "No fish yet. The landlady brought in some melon to eat. Water too cold for swimming."

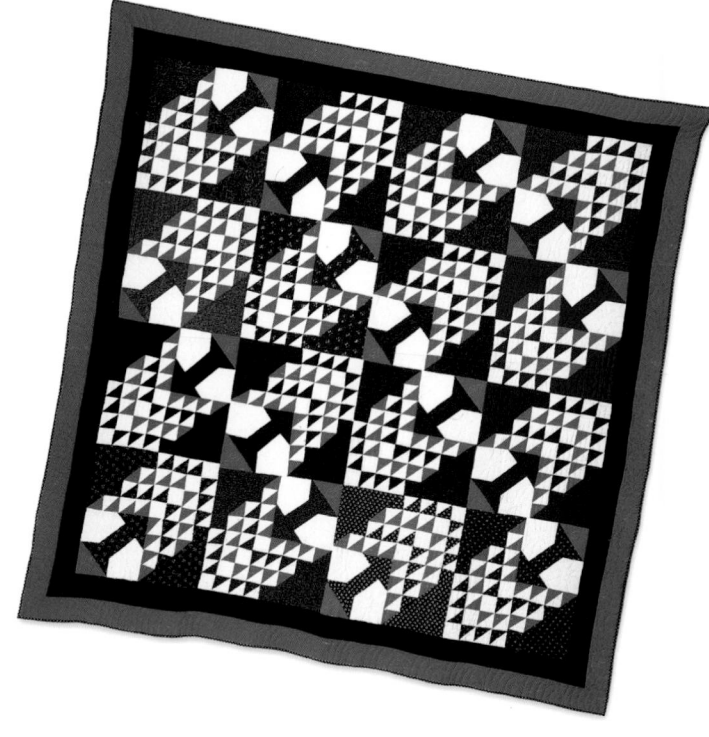

Tree of Paradise by Barbara Brackman, Lawrence, Kansas, 1983-1996. Quilted by Didi Sulvatierri. Collection of Pamela Rugen. Pine trees are a popular design. I copied this one from an antique quilt for my niece.

Augusta	*New England Block*	*Pine Forest*
Maine Woods	*Maine's Spreading Pine Tree*	*Pine Burr*

The pine tree image has been a favorite of quilters for more than a century. *Workbasket* magazine chose a traditional pattern and named it **Maine's Spreading Pine Tree** for its All-State Quilt in 1935. About the same time, Ruby Short McKim chose the **Pine Forest** for Maine in her syndicated column, *Patchwork Parade of States*. Pine trees are so important to Maine's image that even the state flower is the White Pine Cone and Tassel. Pine Cone or **Pine Burr** is an old name for a pattern popular in the mid-nineteenth century. This one is from Clara Stone's *Practical Needlework: Quilt Patterns*, one of the earliest quilt pattern catalogs.

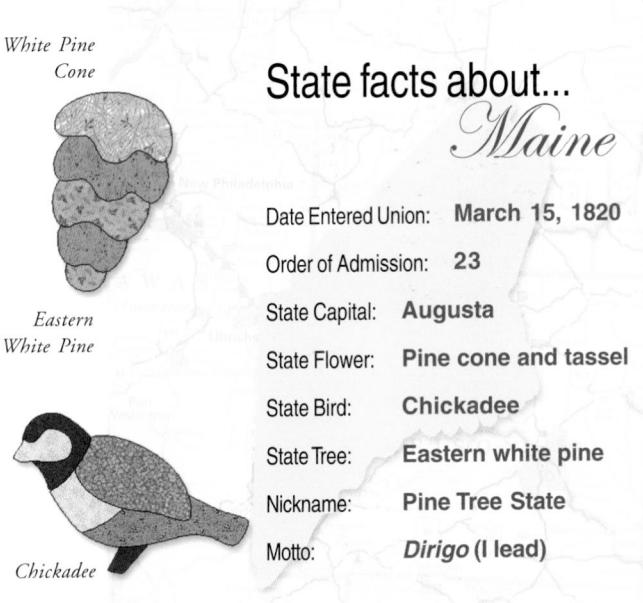

White Pine Cone

Eastern White Pine

Chickadee

State facts about...
Maine

Date Entered Union:	**March 15, 1820**
Order of Admission:	**23**
State Capital:	**Augusta**
State Flower:	**Pine cone and tassel**
State Bird:	**Chickadee**
State Tree:	**Eastern white pine**
Nickname:	**Pine Tree State**
Motto:	***Dirigo* (I lead)**

Maryland
Old Line State

The State of Maryland was 350 years old on March 25, 1984,
the anniversary of settlers' first landing at St. Clement's Island in 1634.
Cecil Calvert, Lord Baltimore, had been granted a charter two years earlier.

The new colony was named by England's King Charles I for his wife Henrietta Maria. Thus a **Queen's Crown** is the first in our sampler of Maryland patterns. **Maryland** was the state's entry in the 1907 *Hearth and Home* contest for state blocks. And **Annapolis** was in the same magazine's state capital contest a few years later.

Since Maryland was the first British colony to legislate religious freedom in the new world, remember the state's nickname, The Free State, with **Cross and Crown** from *Orange Judd Farmer* (September 1900 issue). Maryland is also called The Old Line State because during the Revolutionary War its

Cross and Crown

soldiers were known as the Maryland Line. George Washington considered them a major factor in the 1776 Battle of Long Island victory. Other generals depended on Maryland soldiers during the battles at Princeton, Staten Island, and in the Carolinas. So I've

included **Soldier's March** in this state's blocks to commemorate these brave Marylanders. This pattern comes from a Carroll County, Maryland, quilt shown in the book, *Once Upon A Quilt*, by Celine Mahler.

During the War of 1812, Maryland contributed something special to the new nation. Francis Scott Key, an attorney from Frederick, wrote his "Star-Spangled Banner" during the battle for Baltimore at Fort McHenry on September 14, 1814. A 1941 *Kansas City Star* pattern, **The Star Spangled Banner**, commemorates Key's anthem.

The Star Spangled Banner

Though the hymn appeared in a local newspaper a week after Key wrote it, the song did not become the official United States National Anthem until 1931.

By the time of the Civil War, another Marylander – Barbara Fritchie – was immortalized in a poem by John Greenleaf Whittier. On September 10, 1862, Fritchie confronted Confederate troops in her native Frederick, shouting the classic line "Shoot, if you must, this old grey head, but spare your country's flag." The block **Barbara Fritchie Star** is from a *Needlecraft* magazine clipping that describes it as a star pattern found on a quilt in the Fritchie home.

Barbara Fritchie Star

Moon Over the Mountain recalls the Blue Ridge Mountains in western Maryland. Eastern Maryland is usually recognized for its beaches and waterways. A traditional quilt pattern called Birds In the Air is known as **Wave On the Ocean** in Maryland, where the Chesapeake Bay and Atlantic Ocean have such a great influence. The pattern's many triangles resemble other sawtooth patterns, such as **Maryland Beauty** shown in Hinson's *A Quilter's Companion*. That block resembles an old-time favorite, **Sailboat**, which recalls the great expanse of Chesapeake Bay waters and also reminds us that the United States Naval Academy is located in Annapolis. **Baltimore Belle**, from Clara A. Stone's 1906 *Practical Needlework: Quilt Patterns*, suggests not only Maryland's

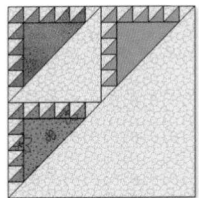

Maryland Beauty

Maryland   *Annapolis*   *Moon Over the Mountain*

Wave on the Ocean   *Sailboat*   *Black-eyed Susan*

Queen's Crown   *Soldier's March*   *Washington Sidewalk*

large port city but also the "fascinating ladies" of Baltimore who, in the mid-nineteenth century, produced the beautiful appliqué quilts known as Baltimore Bride or Baltimore Album Quilts.

Baltimore Belle

Southern Star, from *Hearth and Home*, reminds us that Maryland is just below the Mason-Dixon Line surveyed in 1763-1767. A Ladies Art Company pattern, **Washington Sidewalk**, reminds us that Maryland ceded some of its land on March 30, 1791, to provide a site for the newly founded nation's capital, Washington, District of Columbia.

Southern Star

A pieced **Black-Eyed Susan**, from *Capper's Weekly*, reminds us not only of the state flower but also of the Black-Eyed Susan wreath awarded the winner at The Preakness, the middle jewel of horse racing's Triple Crown, held yearly at Baltimore's Pimlico Race Course.

written by Louise O. Townsend

State facts about...

Maryland

ate Entered Union: **April 28, 1788**

der of Admission: **7**

ate Capital: **Annapolis**

ate Flower: **Black-eyed Susan**

ate Bird: **Baltimore oriole**

ate Tree: **White oak**

ckname: **Old Line State; Free State**

tto: *Fatti maschii, parole femine* (Manly deeds, womanly words); *Scuto bono voluntatis tuae coronasti nos* (With favor wilt Thou compass us as with a shield)

Black-eyed Susan

White Oak

Baltimore Oriole

81

Massachusetts
Bay State

Massachusetts has played an important role in American history from the earliest days. In print, the name dates to 1614, when John Smith recorded Massachuset as an Indian village.

The word derives from Mass-adchu-seuck, the people from the big hill. An **Indian Star** can recall those Big Hill People.

The **Mayflower** (a) is one of Maryland's important historical symbols. A 1936 pattern from the *Kansas City Star* remembers this ship that transported the first English settlers

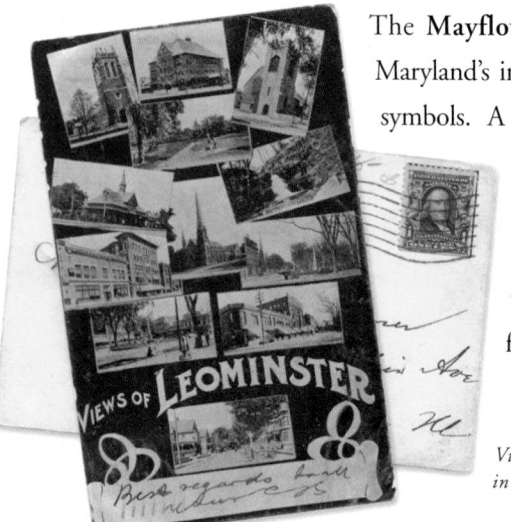

Views of Leominster in 1906.

to Plymouth Rock. The ship's name became the state flower, which can be pieced in a stylized **Mayflower** (b), syndicated by the Laura Wheeler column in the 1930s. Other pieced Mayflowers are (c) from Mrs. Danner's Quilts in 1970 and (d) the Ladies Art Company pattern catalog about 1890.

Indian Star

Massachusetts was at the heart of our Revolutionary War, becoming one of the original 13 states. **Massachusetts** is from *Hearth and Home's* state series. Mrs. T.W.F. of Taunton mailed the block to the magazine, suggesting it might make a "very pretty album quilt-block, the name and

Mayflower (a) Mayflower (b) Mayflower (c)

Mayflower (d) Boston Commons Boston Pavement

Boston Corners (a) Boston Corners (b) Boston Puzzle

Modern Priscilla. Other old-fashioned, Anglo-Saxon names like Nancy Page and Nancy Cabot (pseudonyms for Florence LaGanke and Loretta Leitner Rising), headed national quilt pattern columns.

Hearth and Home remembered **Boston**, the capital of the Commonwealth (for Massachusetts is technically not a state). "L.M.R." contributed the block and said it should be made in three colors. "For the light portions I use bleached muslin, pieces of which accumulate

Boston

when underclothing is made at home." Boston's city plan is recalled in several designs. **Boston Commons** is from Mountain Mist. Nancy Cabot showed two variations of the simple diamond design as **Boston Corners** (a,b). **Boston Pavement** is from the *Farmer's Wife* magazine. And **Boston Puzzle** is from the Ladies Art Company catalog in the late nineteenth century.

address of the friend who pieces it, or who furnishes scraps of her dresses to make it, being written on the white strips."

Massachusetts

Massachusetts Priscilla was *Workbasket's* state entry in their 1935 All-State Quilt. The pattern reflects the Colonial Revival, a fashion trend emphasizing New England heritage and design. Quilts were such an important part of the Colonial look that many patterns were given long pedigrees, having little to do with historic truth. Priscilla Alden,

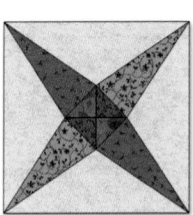

Massachusetts Priscilla

and her triangular romance with Miles Standish and John Alden, was a heroine whose name echoed colonial authenticity. One of the leading early twentieth-century needlework magazines was named

Mayflower

American Elm

Chickadee

State facts about...
Massachusetts

Date Entered Union:	**February 6, 1788**
Order of Admission:	**6**
State Capital:	**Boston**
State Flower:	**Mayflower**
State Bird:	**Chickadee**
State Tree:	**American Elm**
Nickname:	**Bay State**
Motto:	*Ense petit placidam sub libertate quietem* (By the sword we seek peace, but peace only under liberty)

Michigan
Wolverine State

Michigan's name is a variation of Michi-guma, the Chippewa word for "great lake." Lake Michigan and the other Great Lakes are among the state's prime industrial and recreational assets.

We can find many Michigan patterns in old magazines. During the first decades of the twentieth century, *Hearth & Home* magazine asked readers to "send in their choicest patterns for illustration," urging them "to try to originate designs." Readers responded with **Michigan**, **Michigan Beauty**, and **Lansing**, named for the state capital. And in 1940, *Farm Journal* published **Michigan Favorite**.

Michigan

In the 1930s, Ruby McKim chose **Arrowheads** for Michigan in her "Patchwork Parade of States," syndicated to newspapers country-wide. That design paid tribute to the many Indian tribes who had lived near Michi-guma. *Workbasket* magazine's 1935 All-State Quilt also recalled the Indians, with **Michigan's Pontiac Star**, named for an eighteenth-century Ottawa chief who fought British rule, and who was remembered generations later by a Detroit automobile designer.

The pattern that Hearth and Home called Michigan Beauty was also sold by the Newcomb Loom Works. These small trade cards from about 1900 are particularly collectible.

Michigan Beauty	*Lansing*	*Arrowheads*
Michigan's Pontiac Star	*Apple Tree*	*Pride of Holland*
Historic Oak Leaf	*The Pine Tree Quilt Design*	*Michigan Favorite*

A crowd of Edwardian funlovers in a hand-colored postcard.

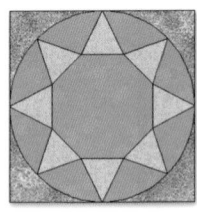

The Car Wheel

Automobiles come to mind when people say Michigan. Make this connection in your Michigan quilt by piecing the **The Car Wheel**, printed in the *Kansas City Star* in 1940. Michigan is famous for other products as well. The state leads the country in cherry production; remember Michigan cherries with a **Cherry Basket**, from Ladies Art Company catalog in the 1890s. Or honor Michigan's hardwood forests with **Historic Oak Leaf** from the Illinois State Register in 1932, during the time when an oak furniture suite from Grand Rapids was the dream of every bride.

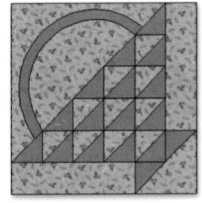

Cherry Basket

Michigan's official state tree is the white pine. From the many, many pine tree block designs popular over the last century, I've chosen **The Pine Tree Quilt Design** from *Wallace's Farmer* in 1928. Or, use another tree – Nancy Cabot's **Apple Tree** with red patches symbolizing the apples among the green leaves – in honor of the state flower, the apple blossom. Although it's not the state flower, the tulip and the town that grows them can be represented by **Pride of Holland** from *Farm Journal*.

State facts about... *Michigan*

Apple Blossom

White Pine Cone

Robin

Date Entered Union:	**January 26, 1837**
Order of Admission:	**26**
State Capital:	**Lansing**
State Flower:	**Apple blossom**
State Bird:	**Robin**
State Tree:	**Eastern white pine**
Nickname:	**Wolverine State, Lady of the Lake**
Motto:	*Si quaeris peninsulam amoenam circumspice* (If you seek a pleasant peninsula, look about you)

85

Minnesota

North Star State

The name Minnesota is one of the most romantic of state names.
The syllables speak to us of the Native Americans who lived there for centuries
before European explorers and settlers came to call it the Land of 10,000 Lakes.

Minnesota indirectly owes its present name to Henry Schoolcraft, who lived with the Ojibwa in the Upper Great Lakes region before the West was opened. Schoolcraft studied Indian culture carefully, and heard the beauty in their language. It was he who encouraged Congress to retain native names for American features and places, so we have today Nebraska, Oklahoma, and Minnesota rather than New Sweden or New Prussia.

Minnesota (a)

George R. Stewart, in his book *Names On the Land*, traces the meaning of Minnesota to Cloudy Water, for the turbid Mississippi River. The words were later interpreted to refer to clouds – and thus Sky Blue Water.

One block named **Minnesota** (a) is from the 1930's Nancy Page syndicated newspaper column. An earlier **Minnesota** (b) is from a series of state patterns that *Hearth and Home* magazine ran in the early twentieth century. The magazine also invited readers to send patterns named for state capitals, and published **St. Paul**. *Workbasket* magazine designed an All-State Quilt in 1935, choosing the **Blazing Star of Minnesota** for the North Star State. Stars pieced of diamonds are popular with Lakota Indian quiltmakers from Minnesota and other states, so it was an especially appropriate choice.

Minnesota (b)

Although no traditional patterns symbolize Minnesota as the Gopher State, many blocks remind us of its other nicknames. **North Star** (a) is from the Lockport Batting Company's pattern series, **North Star** (b) is from the 1930s Laura Wheeler syndicated pattern service, and **The North Star** was sent to the *Kansas City Star* in 1947. Quilters in The Land of 10,000 Lakes can be remembered with **Lady of the Lake** (a) from *Hearth and Home* or with the Ladies Art Company **Lady of the Lake** (b) pattern of the 1890s.

Today, many of us think of Minnesota as home to Norwegian bachelor farmers, thanks to Garrison Keillor's radio stories about his home state on "A Prairie Home Companion." Two patterns can

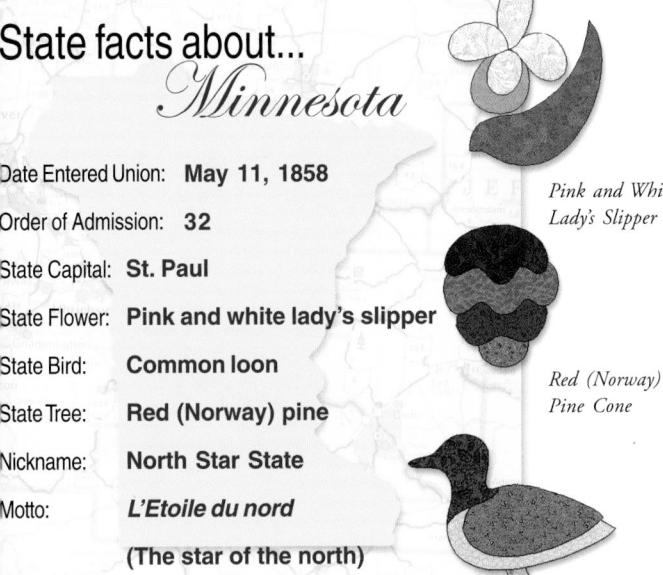

Lady of the Lake by Carol Gilham Jones, Lawrence, Kansas, 1976.

Lady of the Lake (a)

St. Paul   Blazing Star of Minnesota   Lady of the Lake (b)

North Star (a)   North Star (b)   The North Star

Bachelor's Puzzle (a)   Bachelor's Puzzle (b)   Ducks and Ducklings

represent those stalwarts of the prairie. **Bachelor's Puzzle** (a) was in the *Kansas City Star* in 1931 and **Bachelor's Puzzle** (b) was in the *Oklahoma Farmer Stockman* the same year. You can't celebrate bachelor farmers, however, without giving credit to the **Farmer's Wife**, a 1932 *Kansas City Star* pattern. This block also reminds us of a magazine by that name, published in St. Paul from the nineteenth century to 1939. The *Farmer's Wife* offered numerous quilt patterns in those years, among them **Pine Tree**, which can represent the state tree. The state bird is the loon, a black and white waterfowl. **Ducks and Ducklings**, in black and white on a sky blue background, can represent the loons with their wonderful cry. The pattern comes from Ruth Finley's 1929 book, *Old Patchwork Quilts and the Women Who Made Them.*

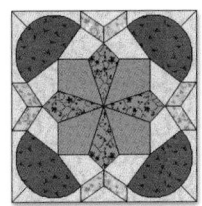

Farmer's Wife

Pine Tree

State facts about...
Minnesota

Date Entered Union: **May 11, 1858**

Order of Admission: **32**

State Capital: **St. Paul**

State Flower: **Pink and white lady's slipper**

State Bird: **Common loon**

State Tree: **Red (Norway) pine**

Nickname: **North Star State**

Motto: ***L'Etoile du nord***

   (The star of the north)

Pink and White Lady's Slipper

Red (Norway) Pine Cone

Common Loon

Mississippi

by Sharon Vesecky, Baldwin, Kansas, 2001.
Machine-pieced and appliquéd, machine-quilted. Sharon pieced Hearth and Home's Mississippi,
and bordered it with mockingbirds and 3-dimensional magnolias.

Mississippi
Magnolia State

Historians estimate that when European explorers landed
on the southern Mississippi coast, 30,000 Native Americans
lived in what is now the state.

The three most powerful tribes were the Chickasaw, Choctaw, and the Natchez, but no patterns have been named specifically for them or any of Mississippi's other tribes. Most had long been relocated to Indian Territory in Oklahoma when

"In this house Henry Wadsworth Longfellow wrote, 'The Building of the Ship.'"

books and magazines began recording quilt pattern names. But we can recall Mississippi's first residents with **Indian Trail** from the *Kansas City Star* in 1931.

Mississippi was named for the river, one of the world's longest. Most explanations attribute the name to the Algonquian language, a combination of words that means "Big River." **Mississippi** is the name of a quilt pattern from *Hearth and Home* magazine in the first decades of

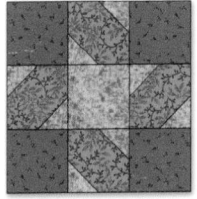

Mississippi

this century. *Hearth and Home* also printed a **Mississippi Daisy**, and Clara Stone published **Mississippi Oak Leaf** in a 1906 pamphlet. *Needlecraft* magazine printed **Mississippi Pink** in 1929.

The first Europeans to colonize Mississippi were led by the LeMoyne family. Pierre LeMoyne

Star of LeMoyne

settled Old Biloxi (now Ocean Springs) in 1699. Remember the family with a **Star of LeMoyne**, one of the oldest patchwork patterns, and a name recorded by Ruth Finley in her 1929 book, *Old Patchwork Quilts and the Women Who Made Them*. **Biloxi** has a pattern named for it, one that quilt historian Cuesta Benberry has traced to *Scribner's* magazine in 1894.

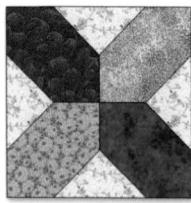
The Cotton Boll Quilt

Mississippi became the twentieth state in 1817, as cotton production was developing into the South's major crop. Mississippi cotton crops expanded to supply mills in the northern states and Europe. The abundance caused fabric prices to drop so low that many American women could afford the luxury of buying cotton fabrics especially for their quilts. It is no

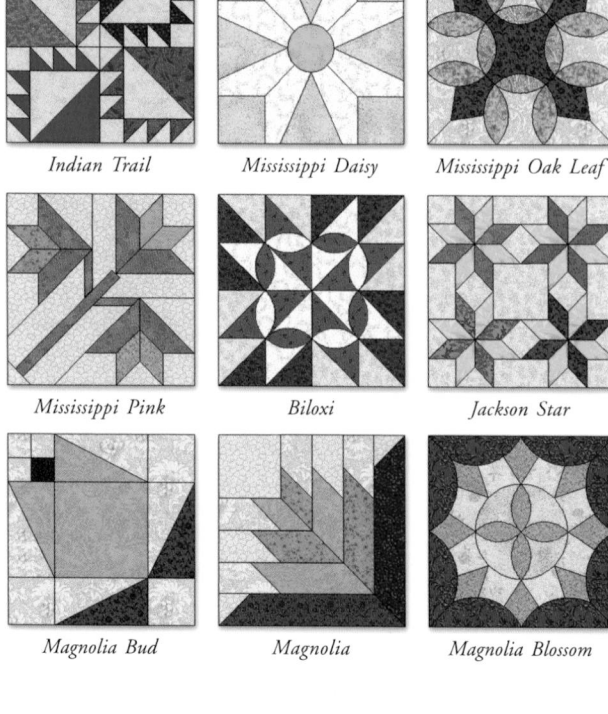

Indian Trail *Mississippi Daisy* *Mississippi Oak Leaf*

Mississippi Pink *Biloxi* *Jackson Star*

Magnolia Bud *Magnolia* *Magnolia Blossom*

wonder there are patterns named to celebrate the cotton plant. **The Cotton Boll Quilt** pattern appeared in a 1941 *Kansas City Star*.

The state capital is **Jackson**, the name of a block from *Hearth and Home*. Somehow Jackson, Miss. was switched to Miss Jackson when the Ladies Art Company added the pattern to their mail order catalog

Jackson

in the 1920s, so the design goes by both names. A **Jackson Star** appeared in the *Kansas City Star* in 1931, a different way of looking at the Star of LeMoyne.

Mississippi's magnificent magnolia is the state flower and the state tree. **Magnolia Bud** is from the *Kansas City Star* in 1932, and **Magnolia** is from the syndicated columnist Laura Wheeler at about the same time. **Magnolia Blossom**, from the *Oklahoma Farmer and Stockman* in 1930, is a challenging pieced design.

State facts about...
Mississippi

Magnolia Flower

Magnolia Tree

Mockingbird

Date Entered Union:	**December 10, 1817**
Order of Admission:	**20**
State Capital:	**Jackson**
State Flower:	**Magnolia**
State Bird:	**Mockingbird**
State Tree:	**Magnolia**
Nickname:	**Magnolia State**
Motto:	**Virtute et armis**
	(By valor and arms)

90

Missouri
Show-Me State

Missouri is well-known as the home of Mark Twain, Jesse James and Harry Truman. But to quilt pattern collectors, Missouri is best remembered as the home of four major quilt design sources: the *Kansas City Star*, Ruby McKim Studios, Aunt Martha Studios and the Ladies Art Company.

The *Kansas City Star* published hundreds of original quilt block patterns from 1928 to 1960. Ruby McKim, of Independence, began the *Star's* quilt pattern column in 1928. Her patterns were also syndicated by numerous other newspapers. McKim also published several pattern catalogs. Aunt Martha, another name for the Colonial Pattern Company, published

Missouri

catalogs and *Workbasket* magazine from Kansas City. The Ladies Art Company, of St. Louis, collected popular quilt block designs and sold the patterns through catalogs beginning about 1889.

Since Missouri had so many quilt pattern sources, it's not surprising to find many Missouri block designs. Eveline Foland, who followed McKim as a designer at the *Kansas City Star*, named **Old**

"A well-dressed child from Moberly, Missouri, in 1887."

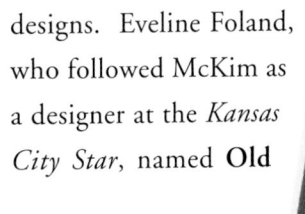

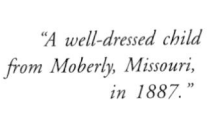

91

Jesse James home in St. Joseph, Missouri. Bushwhacker turned post-war outlaw, Jesse James, remains a Civil War hero in western Missouri.

Missouri Puzzle (a)

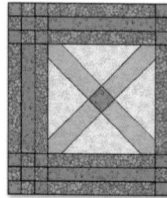

Missouri Puzzle (b)

Missouri Puzzle (c)

Missouri Star (a)

Missouri Star (b)

St. Louis Star

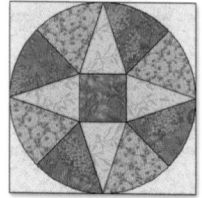

Missouri Morning Star

St. Louis Block

St. Louis

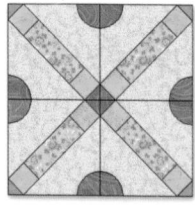

Old Missouri

Missouri and **Missouri Puzzle** (a). The Ladies Art Company sold their own **Missouri Puzzle** (b). Clara Stone had another **Missouri Puzzle** (c). The *Kansas City Star* featured a **Missouri Star** (a) in 1930. And Nancy Cabot's column in the *Chicago Tribune* included another **Missouri Star** (b) in 1933.

Missouri Daisy

Aunt Martha Studios offered a **Missouri Daisy**, a variation of a similar block with gathered petals from the *Kansas City Star*. The *Kansas City Star's* last pieced Missouri pattern was **Missouri Morning Star** in 1950.

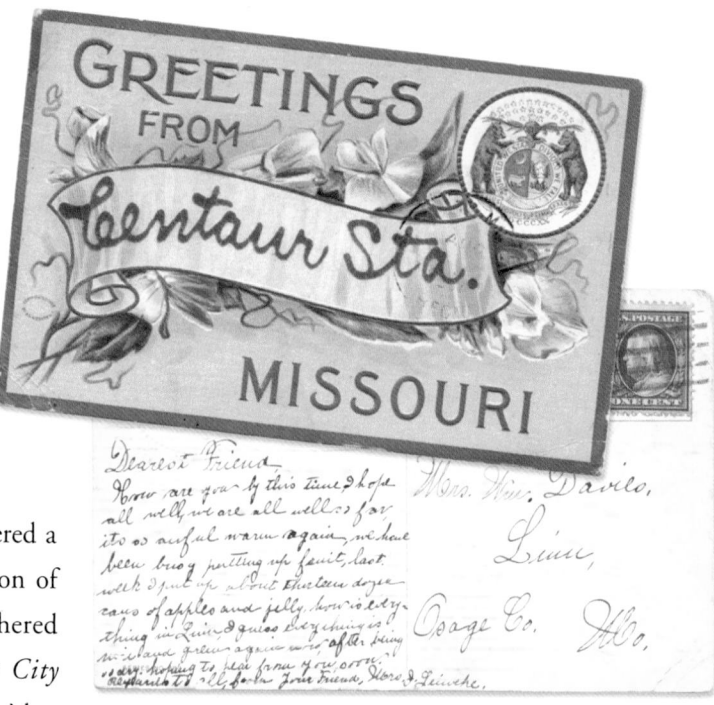

A 1911 message chronicles summer in Missouri. "It's so awful warm again. We have been putting up fruit, last week I put up about thirteen dozen cans of apples and jelly."

Missouri Star by Josephine Maes and Sadie Smith, about 1935.

Carthage, Missouri, 1909.

The Jabe Moore family, about 1910.

Jefferson City

Dogwood

Hearth and Home included **Missouri** in their series of state patterns and **Jefferson City** in the one on state capitals. The Ladies Art Company named two patterns in honor of its home town – **St Louis Star** and **St Louis Block**. Carlie Sexton included **St Louis** in her 1930 pamphlet.

The state tree is the Dogwood. Remember it with a pieced **Dogwood** from the Laura Wheeler syndicated column.

Hawthorn

Flowering Dogwood

Bluebird

State facts about...
Missouri

Date Entered Union:	**August 10, 1821**
Order of Admission:	**24**
State Capital:	**Jefferson City**
State Flower:	**Hawthorn**
State Bird:	**Bluebird**
State Tree:	**Dogwood**
Nickname:	**Show-Me State**
Motto:	*Salus populi suprema lex esto* (The welfare of the people shall be the supreme law)

Montana

Big Sky Country

The name Montana is one of the prettiest of the American states.
Congress, when it named the Montana Territory, interpreted the word to mean
"mountainous" in Spanish, but the word, like Indiana, is latinized English.

The name Montana fits the state well, or at least Montana's western one-third. For that topography, use a **Rocky Mountain Puzzle** from a 1933 Nancy Cabot column in the *Chicago Tribune*. The pattern includes an abtract log cabin surrounded by mountain peaks, a good combination to honor Montana's early settlers. To recall the eastern two-thirds of the state: a **Prairie Sunrise** from *Hearth and Home*.

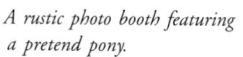

A rustic photo booth featuring a pretend pony.

The Montana pattern block first appeared in *Hearth and Home* magazine's state series. In 1907 the editors asked readers to submit designs for each state. Mrs. G.N.C. of Springdale, Montana, sent a pattern, which she pictured as an octagon set with four pointed stars. With the addition of some corner triangles it becomes a more conventional square **Montana** block. *Hearth and Home* sometimes printed two designs for a state; **Montana Star** was a second entry in the series. In the 1930s the *Chicago Tribune's* Nancy Cabot column published **Montana Maze.**

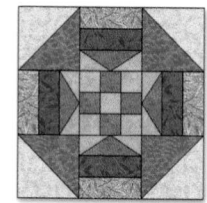

Montana

Other magazines also ran state series patterns. In 1935, *Workbasket* designed an All-State Quilt, choosing **Fifty-Four Forty or Fight** for Montana. This

Prairie Sunrise · Montana Maze · Fifty-Four Forty or Fight

Helena · Pine Burr · Gold and Silver

Rocky Mountain Puzzle · Montana Star · Custer's Last Stand

Montana's official tree, the ponderosa pine, offers many pattern possibilities. **Pine Tree** is from a 1934 *Kansas City Star*. **Pine Burr**, another name for pine cone, is a popular nineteenth-century design, recorded by Clara Stone in 1906.

Pine Tree

The state's motto, "Oro y plata," means gold and silver. A **Gold and Silver** pattern was published in the Nancy Cabot column. **Gold Nuggets** is a variation of the spool design in which the outer pieces are scraps, the center squares yellow. It appeared in *Aunt Kate's Quilting Bee*, a 1960's pattern magazine. Either design could

Gold Nuggets

represent the mineral wealth of Montana, known as The Treasure State, but more commonly called the Big Sky Country, since most of its residents consider Montana scenery its true treasure.

pattern is an old design with a political name that may date back to the 1844 presidential election, when James Polk's supporters adopted that slogan to show their enthusiasm for western expansion up to the 54th parallel, territory that included what is now Montana.

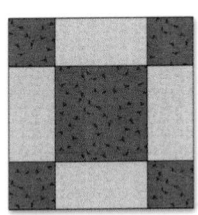

The Sheepfold Quilt

Ruby McKim's *Patchwork Parade of States* newspaper column in the '30s symbolized Montana and its sheep ranches with the Nine-Patch that is sometimes called **The Sheepfold Quilt**. The state capital, **Helena**, was honored with a string star pattern in *Hearth and Home's* state capital series around 1910.

On the plains, in the Crow Reservation, is the Custer Battlefield Monument, commemorating the 1876 battle near the Little Big Horn River. When General Custer's widow died in 1933, the Nancy Cabot column remembered the battle with **Custer's Last Stand**, a pattern recalling the tragedy of the Indian Wars.

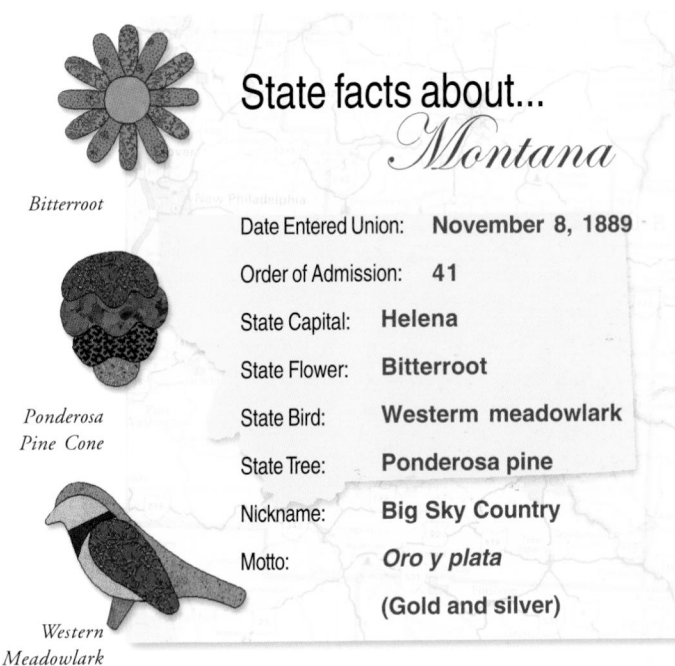

Bitterroot

Ponderosa Pine Cone

Western Meadowlark

State facts about...
Montana

Date Entered Union:	**November 8, 1889**
Order of Admission:	**41**
State Capital:	**Helena**
State Flower:	**Bitterroot**
State Bird:	**Western meadowlark**
State Tree:	**Ponderosa pine**
Nickname:	**Big Sky Country**
Motto:	***Oro y plata***
	(Gold and silver)

Nebraska
Cornhusker State

Nebraska had long been Indian territory, named initially
for the Indian words Ni-bthaska, the wide river called the Platte today.
In the mid-nineteenth century, the United States reserved land near the Platte
for both native and immigrant tribes.

*I*ndian **Meadow** is an old pattern, given that new name about 1930 by *Woman's World* magazine. Recall those days when Plains Indians and buffalo dominated the country from the Missouri River to the Sand Hills. Celebrate the landscape with **Sandhills Star**, sent to the *Kansas City Star* in 1939 by Myrtle Timblin Ogden of Lamar.

An unusual outfit and an unusual pose from the Bon Ton photo studios in Lincoln, about 1890.

Non-native people, forbidden to settle until 1854, followed the Platte River through the Sand Hills on their way to the Oregon Territory and California. To remember the Great River Road, include a block of the **Road to California** pattern, a popular design in the years of western migration. The name was recorded by the Ladies Art Company about 1890.

About 1910, *Hearth and Home* magazine asked readers to mail in patterns named for their home states. M.E. Bradford, editor of the "Useful and Fanciwork" page, admitted she could not

An old newspaper clipping showing State of Nebraska (a).

96

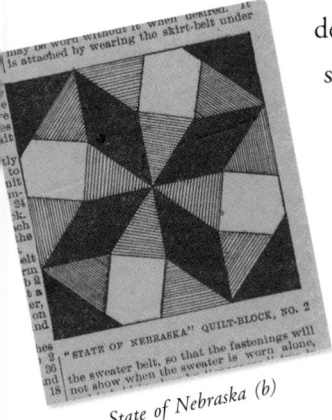

State of Nebraska (b)

decide between two entries, so she published both **State of Nebraska** block patterns (a & b). Two decades later, Nancy Cabot added a little more detail for her version of **Nebraska**, obviously drawn from the *Hearth and Home* pattern.

Nebraska became a state just in time to benefit from the Homestead Act, granting land to those who would farm it, including European immigrants looking for their own land. Ruby Short McKim remembered Nebraska's women homesteaders with **Prairie Queen** in her *Patchwork Parade of States*, syndicated in newspapers in the early 1930s.

Settlers changed the landscape with farms and ranches, and with windmills providing power for water wells. Nebraska's wind power is symbolized

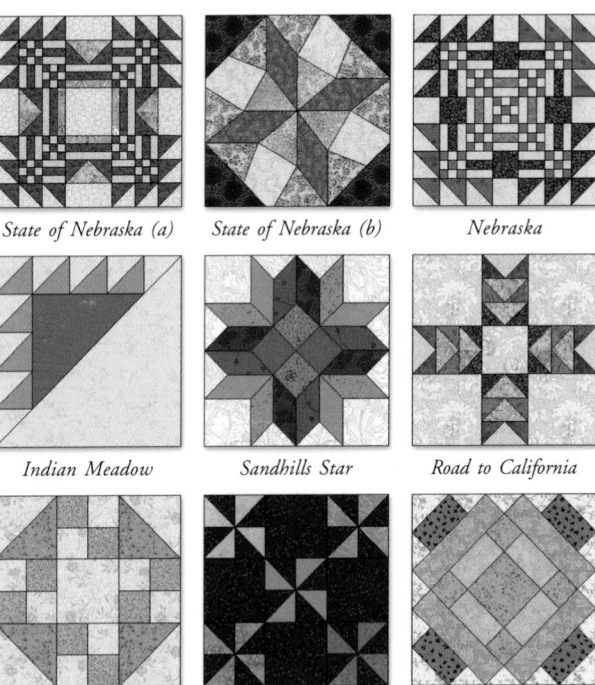

State of Nebraska (a)   State of Nebraska (b)   Nebraska

Indian Meadow   Sandhills Star   Road to California

Prairie Queen   Windmill   Lincoln

in an early design named **Windmill** in a 1903 *Ladies' Home Journal* article. The state's capital, **Lincoln**, was honored with a variation of the traditional album block, sent by a reader of *Hearth and Home*.

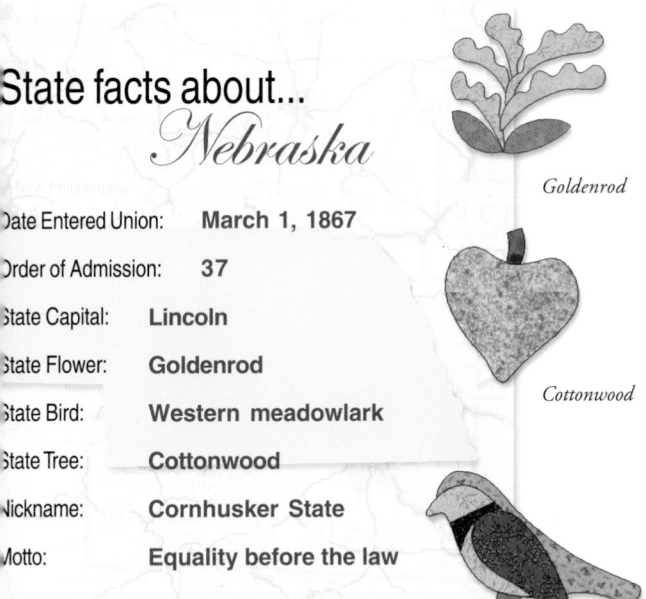

State facts about...
Nebraska

Date Entered Union:	**March 1, 1867**
Order of Admission:	**37**
State Capital:	**Lincoln**
State Flower:	**Goldenrod**
State Bird:	**Western meadowlark**
State Tree:	**Cottonwood**
Nickname:	**Cornhusker State**
Motto:	**Equality before the law**

Goldenrod

Cottonwood

Western Meadowlark

One could make a nice collection of state hospital post cards.

Nevada

Silver State

During the Civil War, Nevada's mineral wealth made it so valuable
to the Union that Congress named it the 36th state,
a history recalled in one nickname, "The Battle Born State."

Nevada (a) is the state design in *Hearth and Home* magazine's state pattern series.

Silver and Gold

In the 1930s, *Workbasket* magazine published an All-State Quilt with a second block called **Nevada** (b). The pattern they chose also was called Goldbrick; if the corners are properly shaded, gold ingots are visible. **Silver and Gold** also celebrates two of the state's prized natural resources. The pattern appeared in *Needlecraft Magazine* in 1929.

Carson City, the state capital named for frontiersman Kit Carson, was settled during the silver boom. The pattern is from *Hearth and Home*. Mining remains important to the economy, but tourism is Nevada's biggest industry. In the 1930s, Ruby McKim designed a *Patchwork Parade of States* and chose the old pattern **Wheel of Fortune** to recall Nevada's gambling casinos – a major tourist attraction. To give you a little luck at the tables, include a **Lucky Star** (a) from the Nancy Cabot column in the *Chicago Tribune*,

Carson City

Nevada (a) Nevada (b) Wheel of Fortune

Lucky Star (a) Lucky Star (b) Desert Rose

Sage Bud Bluebirds Tiny Pines

A barn raising in Washoe County, Nevada, in 1876.

or a **Lucky Star** (b) from the Laura Wheeler syndicated column that has run in dozens of newspapers since the mid 1930s.

The state's name comes from the Sierra Nevada mountain range. (In Spanish it means "snow-covered mountain range.") The senators naming the territory did not know that little of the range is actually in Nevada. Had they visited, they would have realized that "Nevada," meaning "snowed-upon" or "snowfall," was not a particularly appropriate name for a state that includes the Mojave Desert. You can remember Nevada's true climate with **Desert Rose** from Nancy Cabot.

The state flower is officially the sagebrush, so **Sage Bud** from the *Kansas City Star* in 1930 can celebrate the "Sage Brush State." The state bird is the

Mountain Bluebird. If the diamonds are correctly shaded in the points of the star, **Bluebirds** appear in an old design, renamed by the *Rural New Yorker* farm weekly in 1933. Nevada's tree is the single-leaf piñon pine. Try a **Tiny Pines** block from the syndicated Nancy Page column in the 1930s.

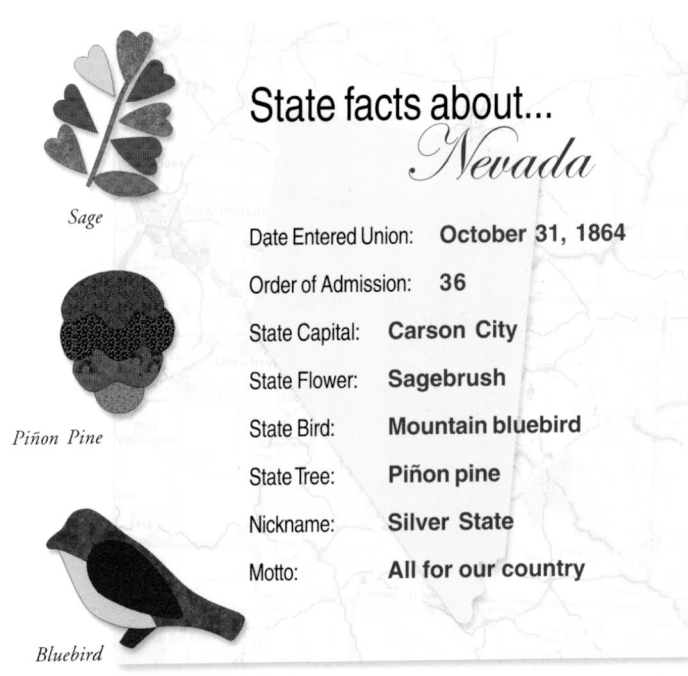

Sage

Piñon Pine

Bluebird

State facts about...
Nevada

Date Entered Union:	**October 31, 1864**
Order of Admission:	**36**
State Capital:	**Carson City**
State Flower:	**Sagebrush**
State Bird:	**Mountain bluebird**
State Tree:	**Piñon pine**
Nickname:	**Silver State**
Motto:	**All for our country**

99

New Hampshire

Granite State

New Hampshire's name comes from Hampshire County in England,
which Captain John Mason left for the American shores, looking for a royal land
grant. The state created from his personal territory was one of the first thirteen,
a state known for its mountains, industries, and historic sites.

A reader of *Hearth and Home* magazine contributed **New Hampshire** to their state series. The state shares this same hexagonal block with Florida. Florida's pattern has only two colors, while New Hampshire's has three. So to keep a tropical tone out of your New England quilt, use three colors in your New Hampshire block.

Hearth and Home reader M. L. W. sent a block called **Concord** for the New Hampshire capital, "an original design which has taken several premiums at fairs." Pattern designer Ruby McKim included **Village School House** for New Hampshire in her *Patchwork Parade of States*, syndicated to newspapers about 1930. The block commemorates New England's indigenous clapboard architecture, and the local emphasis on education.

Concord

"Crawford Notch State Park, New Hampshire. This mountain stream drops over 1000 feet within its mile long descent over the highly inclined ledges of Mt. Webster."

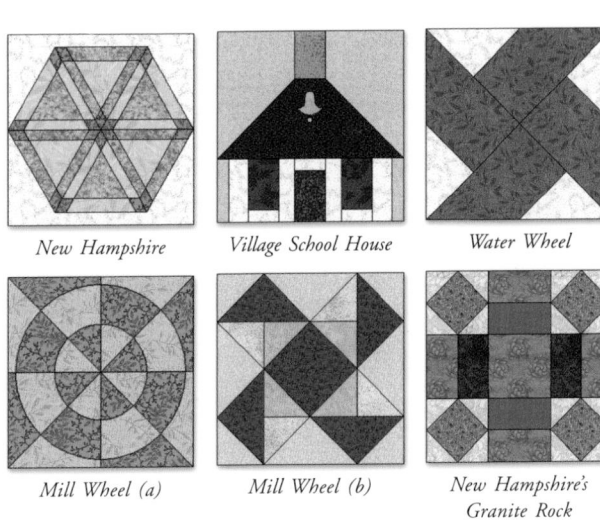

New Hampshire

Village School House

Water Wheel

Mill Wheel (a)

Mill Wheel (b)

New Hampshire's
Granite Rock

State facts about...
New Hampshire

Date Entered Union:	**June 21, 1788**
Order of Admission:	**9**
State Capital:	**Concord**
State Flower:	**Purple lilac**
State Bird:	**Purple finch**
State Tree:	**White birch**
Nickname:	**Granite State**
Motto:	**Live free or die**

Purple Lilac

White Birch

Purple Finch

In the mid-1930s, *Workbasket* magazine published an All-State Quilt with **New Hampshire's Granite Rock** for the Granite State. This pattern is better known as Rolling Stone, a name collected by the Ladies Art Company in the late nineteenth century. It's also quite appropriate for a state known for its "Great Stone Face." New Hampshire is famous for its White Mountains, the highest peaks in New England. Use **Delectable Mountains** from Carrie Hall's 1935 book, *The Romance of the Patchwork Quilt in America*, to honor these beautiful mountains.

Delectable Mountains

Abundant water power was one source of the state's early industrial wealth. **Water Wheel** was named by Marguerite Ickis in *The Standard Book of Quiltmaking and Collecting*. Water power helped create the textile mills which made New Hampshire a source for many of the beautiful cottons that appear in American quilts. To remember the textile mills and their contribution

to our quilt heritage, we have a **Mill Wheel** (a) from the Alice Brooks syndicated newspaper quilt pattern column of the 1930s and another **Mill Wheel** (b) from the *Chicago Tribune's* Nancy Cabot pattern column.

"The Old Man of the Mountains" is a state tourist attraction.

The state tree, the white birch, adds to New England's reputation for fall color.

New Jersey
Garden State

New Jersey, home of Frank Sinatra, Bruce Springsteen and Lucy the giant concrete elephant, might have been named Albania or New Cesarea. Luckily, the English royalty who were given a charter to the region preferred to honor the British Isle of Jersey. Their name endured, while earlier ideas were forgotten.

In 1907, *Hearth and Home's* editor asked readers to name a pattern for their state. The magazine commemorated the Garden State with **New Jersey** (a), a variation of an old album design. The block, with its long strips perfect for signatures, was especially appropriate for New Jersey, because signature quilts with signed blocks were popular there in the mid-nineteenth century.

Rolling Chairs on Boardwalk. Atlantic City, N.J.

From rolling chairs and Miss America through today's casinos, Atlantic City's Boardwalk has been America's most famous.

When I examined signed and dated album quilts from the early 1840s, looking for trends in how the style developed, I found most of the early ones were made along a line from Morristown, New Jersey, south to Baltimore. Quilters who lived along the Delaware River, the border between New Jersey and Pennsylvania, favored signature quilts made of just one patchwork pattern. Quilters who lived further south, especially those in Baltimore, preferred to stitch up a variety of designs into a sampler album. From this area along the Delaware River and the Chesapeake Bay, the fashion spread to other states and territories. By 1870, quilters in the western states and territories were making friendship quilts in the eastern style.

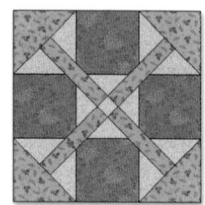

New Jersey (a)

102

Trenton was right at the heart of New Jersey quiltmaking before the Civil War. We can remember those trend-setting women with **Trenton**. Mrs. F.W.V.

Trenton

mailed her design for a block named for the state capital to *Hearth and Home* about 1915. She detailed her philosophy of quiltmaking in her letter. "A quilt is, of course, prettier if made of uniform colors and patterns, but most housekeepers like to use pieces of calico, gingham and white cotton that they have accumulated....I believe in the old-fashioned patchwork quilt, although I make mine up in puffs, tacking, not quilting them."

The syndicated columnist known as Nancy Page (real name: Florence LaGanke Harris) printed a second **New Jersey** (b) design in the 1930s. And Mary McElwain's quilt shop in Wisconsin sold a pattern she called **Jersey Tulip** in that era. The Jersey Tulip is an excellent pattern for a state nicknamed the Garden State. New Jersey may be our most densely populated state, but many rural areas remain. We can also recall the state's

New Jersey (b)	*The Oak Leaf*	*Autumn Leaves*
Jersey Tulip	*Violet Blossoms*	*Liberty Star*
Prosperity Quilt	*Garden Beauty*	*Garden Patch*

nickname with **Garden Beauty** from the Laura Wheeler/ Alice Brooks syndicated column, or **Garden Patch** from Grandma Dexter, another 1930s pattern source.

The red oak is the state tree. Oaks have inspired many block designs, including **The Oak Leaf** from the Illinois State Register in 1932. When Ruby Short McKim designed her 1930s *Patchwork Parade of States*, she included **Autumn Leaves**, representing the state's fall foliage.

New Jersey is one of four states that have picked the purple violet for the official flower. Violets are among the most varied of flowers, with over 300 different types described around the world. Represent the delicate violet blooms in piecework with Robert Frank's **Violet Blossoms**.

The state motto is "Liberty and Prosperity," abstractions that can be represented by **Liberty Star** from the *Kansas City Star* in 1932, and **Prosperity Quilt** from the *Prairie Farmer* magazine a year earlier.

State facts about...
New Jersey

Violet

Red Oak

Goldfinch

Date Entered Union:	**December 18, 1787**
Order of Admission:	**3**
State Capital:	**Trenton**
State Flower:	**Purple violet**
State Bird:	**Eastern goldfinch**
State Tree:	**Red oak**
Nickname:	**Garden State**
Motto:	**Liberty and prosperity**

New Mexico
Land of Enchantment

New Mexico, the Land of Enchantment, celebrates its statehood centennial on January 6, 2012. New Englanders may note that 100 years is not a long time as states go. But New Mexico's history as Indian land, a Spanish and Mexican colony, and an American territory, stretches back for centuries. New Mexico's three cultures, Native American, Spanish, and Anglo, combine to form its character and charm. The New Mexico patterns reflect those three influences.

Symbolize the Native Americans who have occupied pueblos in Taos, Acoma, and other villages for a thousand years with an **Indian Star**, printed in the *Kansas City Star* in 1937, or

Indian Star

an **Indian Mat** from the Nancy Cabot quilt pattern column in the *Chicago Tribune* about the same time. The newspaper quilt columnists of the 1930s occasionally looked to Indian rugs and baskets for design inspiration, as had earlier quilters living among the Indians when New Mexico was a colony and territory.

The Spanish explorer, Coronado, came upon the pueblos in the sixteenth century looking for the "Seven Cities of Gold." He was disappointed to find the gold he sought was just a myth, and instead, the villages were built of adobe that took on a golden glow at sunset. To remember the story of the golden cities, include a **Golden Glow** block, published in Carrie Hall's 1935 book, *The Romance of the Patchwork Quilt in America*.

The Spanish established colonies, with the largest growing up at **Santa Fe**. A quilt block received that name in the early twentieth century, when *Hearth and Home* magazine asked readers to name

Sante Fe

patterns for states and their capitals. Santa Fe, capital for Indian, Spanish, Mexican, and United States governments, had a second block named for it when the Ladies Art Company introduced

Indian Mat	*Golden Glow*	*Sante Fe Block*
Sante Fe Trail	*Texas Star*	*Pine Tree Quilt*

Trail of the Lonesome Pine *Cactus Bloom* *Mexican Star*

a variation in its catalog of quilt designs in the 1910s or '20s. By adding more triangles to *Hearth and Home's* star, they achieved a completely different effect with **Santa Fe Block**.

A few years later, the Nancy Cabot column printed a third variation, calling it **Santa Fe Trail** to honor the road from Missouri to the territorial capital. Begun as a trade route in 1821, the Santa Fe Trail was an important highway carrying gold seekers, pioneers, and settlers (some of whom brought their quilts with them).

Many flags have flown over Santa Fe. When Mexico gained independence from Spain, New Mexico became a Mexican territory – history you can recall with a **Mexican Star** that appeared in Dolores Hinson's 1966 book, *Quilting Manual.* That pattern is also called Sage Bud, perfect for New Mexico's landscape.

The independent country of Texas invaded New Mexico in 1841, so remember the short period of Texas rule with a Lone Star or **Texas Star** from Carrie Hall's book.

A few years later, the United States took possession of the territory. In 1912 it became a state, retaining the name New Mexico. About the time New Mexico became the 47th state in 1912, a *Hearth and Home* reader sent that magazine a **New Mexico** quilt block.

New Mexico

The state tree is the piñon pine, which you can represent with **Pine Tree Quilt** or **Trail of the Lonesome Pine**, both from the Laura Wheeler/Alice Brooks newspaper columns of the 1930s and '40s. The state flower, the Yucca, could be symbolized in **Cactus Bloom** from a 1934 Nancy Cabot column.

New Mexico's industry is based on mining, agriculture, and tourism. But many people believe its greatest product to be its cuisine. If New Mexico makes you think of sopapillas

Corn and Beans

and blue corn enchiladas with green chile sauce, include a **Corn and Beans** block. Try one from Ruth Finley's book, and be sure the corn is blue.

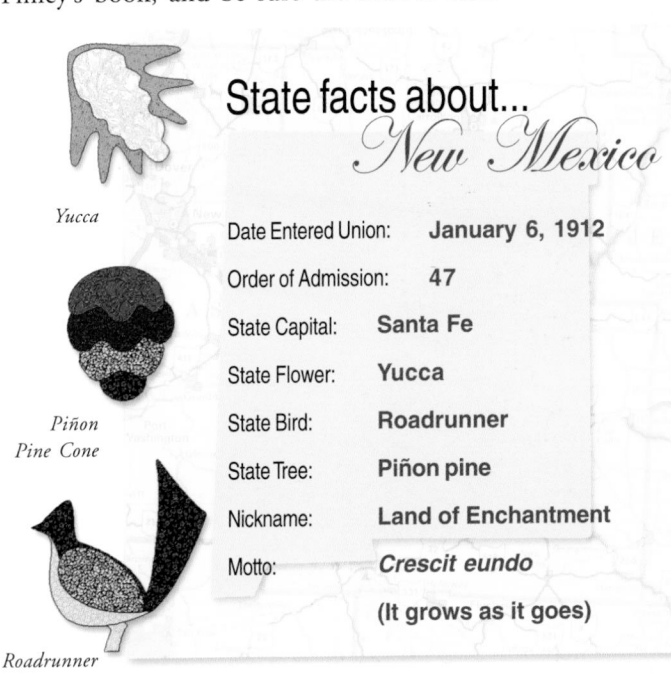

Yucca

Piñon Pine Cone

Roadrunner

State facts about...
New Mexico

Date Entered Union:	**January 6, 1912**
Order of Admission:	**47**
State Capital:	**Santa Fe**
State Flower:	**Yucca**
State Bird:	**Roadrunner**
State Tree:	**Piñon pine**
Nickname:	**Land of Enchantment**
Motto:	*Crescit eundo*
	(It grows as it goes)

New Yawk! New Yawk!
It's so nice I say it twice. (New Joisey ain't bad either...)

by bobbie-frances mcdonald, Lawrence, Kansas, 2001.
Machine-pieced and appliquéd, machine-quilted, hand-beaded. New York Beauty and New Jersey blocks alternate
in this dramatic design. The borders are bobbie-frances' originals, made by adding vines to the corners.
For New York she used the blue bird, wild rose and maple; for New Jersey she used goldfinch, violet and red oak.
Her appliqués are 3-dimensional, including flower leaves and buds she designed on her own.

New York

Empire State

"I ♥ New York" read the bumper stickers; quilters who share the sentiment may want to make a New York quilt with one or more patterns named for the Empire State. Its history is reflected in the patterns. Most were named in the early 1900s by New York's quilters or by syndicated quilt columnists wanting to appeal to them.

Originally, the land around the Hudson and Mohawk River valleys was home to many Indian tribes. The Mohawk people and the river are recalled in the block **Mohawk Trail**. Pattern designer, Ruby McKim, named this sinuous set for a simple fan pattern in

Photo booths were quite popular about 1910.

her *Patchwork Parade of States* series that ran in many newspapers about 1930. The Algonquin Indians are remembered with **Algonquin Trail** (a variation of the popular Rob Peter to Pay Paul design) published by Nancy Cabot in the *Chicago Tribune*. Cabot also honored the Indians (or maybe

Algonquin Trail

it was Manhattan's Algonquin Hotel, a gathering place for literary and theatrical wits of her era) with **Algonquin Charm**.

The Dutch were the first Europeans to colonize the area they called New Amsterdam. The pattern

Mohawk Trail — Algonquin Charm — Knickerbocker Star

Albany — Thousand Islands — Streets of New York

Empire Star — Apple Leaf — Dutch Rose

When quilters think of New York, the pattern that often comes to mind is New York Beauty. In recent years, quilt historians have discovered that the pattern is a traditional Southern design, known as Rocky Mountain or Crown of Thorns. But since Mountain

New York Beauty

Mist sold the pattern as **New York Beauty** in the 1930s, it will remain connected with the Yankee state, despite its Southern roots.

Albany, New York's capital, has a pattern named for it suggested by *Hearth and Home* magazine reader, Mrs. R. J. T. On the northern border of the state, in the St. Lawrence Seaway, are the **Thousand Islands,**

Dutch Rose, from the Ladies Art Company quilt pattern catalog of 1898, recalls this heritage. Today, the rose is New York's official state flower, so a Dutch Rose is particularly appropriate. In 1935, *Workbasket* magazine named a Dutch Rose variation **Knickerbocker Star** in their All-States Quilt design, using a nickname given to the original Dutch colonists' descendants.

State of New York

The British won control of the colony, naming it New York after England's Duke of York. The colony eventually became the **State of New York**, a pattern from *Hearth and Home* magazine's state quilt pattern series. The reader who sent this stars and stripes arrangement may have recalled New York's being the country's first capital after the Revolutionary War.

New York Beauty, by Mary Fischer Boyd, Daly City, California, 1999. We call the pattern New York Beauty. Its traditional name was Rocky Mountain. Mary calls this one Doggy Mountain because she used so many of her ugly fabric "dogs" in the patchwork.

My mother, Cecelia McNally Brackman (center) and her friends at Finnegan's Bar on Long Island during World War II.

for which a quilt pattern (as well as a salad dressing) have been named. Nancy Cabot is responsible for the quilt pattern.

New York City landmarks have several patterns named for them. **Streets of New York** is, like New York Beauty, a combination of pieced block and pieced set. *Good Housekeeping* magazine offered it to readers in 1930. **Herald Square** is from the Nancy Cabot column. The state's official nickname is The Empire State, so I include

Herald Square

Empire Star from *Hearth and Home*. The unofficial nickname for the state's largest city is The Big Apple. **An Apple Leaf** from the *Kansas City Star*, also called Maple Leaf by *Wallace's Farmer* in 1928, symbolizes the nickname and the state's official tree: the Sugar Maple.

View of the Woolworth building when it was "the most prominent landmark of the city."

North Carolina

Tar Heel State

The Carolinas take their name from England's King Charles,
who in 1629 granted a charter for a province which "by the fullness of our power
and kingly authority [we] name the same Carolina."

The colonies eventually split into a North and a South Carolina and became two of the American flag's first thirteen stars. The **Star of North Carolina** appears in the Ladies Art Company's catalog. The block was also known as North Carolina in *Hearth and Home* magazine's state pattern series from the early twentieth century. The *Progressive Farmer*/Nancy Cabot syndicate turned the star a bit and called it **New Star of North Carolina** in the '30s.

Star of North Carolina

North Carolina Lily (a) is a popular pattern. This pieced and appliquéd version was named by Carrie

Hall in her 1935 book, *The Romance of the Patchwork Quilt in America*. Ruby McKim's *Patchwork Parade of States*, syndicated in the 1930s, featured another

Mrs. Barnett sent this card in 1946. "Begin the school for Church Librarians today. I expect to enjoy every minute."

110

North Carolina Lily (b). It seems any variation of these florals (pieced of diamonds) can be named for the Carolinas. Woodard and Greenstein, in their book *Crib Quilts and Other Small Wonders,* showed one **Carolina Lily** (a). And the *Oklahoma Farmer Stockman* showed another (b).

North Carolina Lily (a)	*North Carolina Lily (b)*	*Raleigh*
Carolina Lily (a)	*Carolina Lily (b)*	*Pinecone*
North Carolina Beauty (a)	*North Carolina Beauty (b)*	*New Star of North Carolina*

The *Progressive Farmer*/Nancy Cabot syndicate designed a **North Carolina Beauty** (a). When *Workbasket* magazine sketched an All-State Quilt in 1935, they featured another **North Carolina Beauty** (b). The Laura Wheeler syndicate offered a **Carolina Favorite** about the same time. The state

Carolina Favorite

capital, named for sixteenth-century explorer, Sir Walter Raleigh, was honored by *Hearth and Home* magazine's **Raleigh** block.

North Carolina's state flower is the dogwood. The *Kansas City Star* in 1934 pictured a pieced **Dogwood Blossom** made up of fans and Four-Patches. The state tree is the pine, so a **Pinecone**, also from the *Kansas City Star*, might be a good addition for a patient piecer.

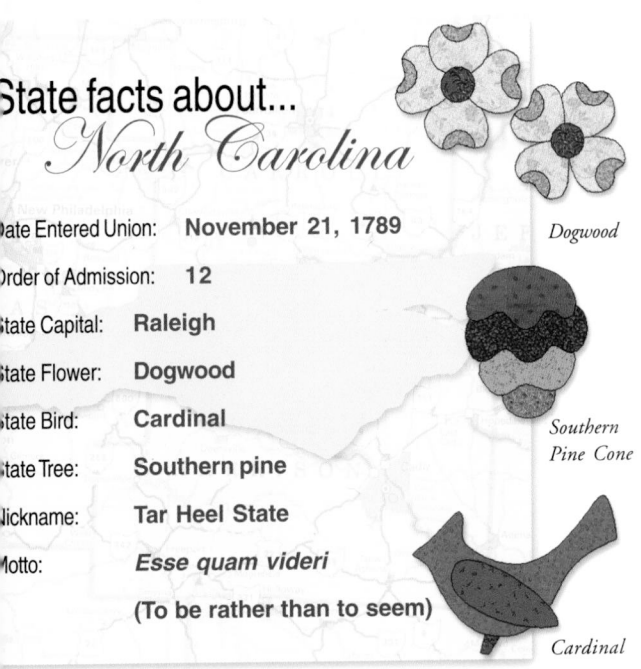

Spirals and Spikes by Bobbi Finley, San Jose, California, 1997. A variation of the Dogwood Blossom.

Dogwood Blossom

111

North Dakota

Peace Garden State

North Dakota was part of the Dakota Territory created in 1861, named for the Native Americans who lived there. By the time the residents were ready for statehood, two distinct areas of settlement had grown up. So two states entered the Union in 1889.

A few decades later, *Hearth and Home* magazine's series of state-named designs included **North Dakota**. The magazine also printed **Bismarck** for North Dakota's capital city. And at some time in the early twentieth century, *Hearth and Home* printed **Dakota Star**, a pattern for North and South Dakota to share.

North Dakota

The region's first settlers were the Indians, among them the tribe we call Sioux, but who called themselves Lakota or Dakota, meaning "friends" or "allied tribes." For the early settlers who gave the state their name, include **Indian Trails**; the name is from Carrie Hall's 1935 book, *The Romance of the Patchwork Quilt in America*. Quilts are an important part of Sioux culture today, especially the star pattterns based on diamonds such as **Prairie Star**. Again, the name is from Carrie Hall.

A normal school was a school for teachers. The State Normal School in Minot, North Dakota, about 1910. The town began as a tent town of the Great Northern Railway in 1886.

French explorers were the first Europeans to claim the land. But France eventually sold it to the U.S. as part of the Louisiana Purchase. Lewis and Clark, sent to explore the country, met Sacagawea in what is now North Dakota. Sacagawea was a Shoshone woman who guided them through the Northwest. To commemorate the first American trip to the Dakotas, make **Lewis and Clark**, a pattern from Clara Stone's 1906 booklet, *Practical Needlework*.

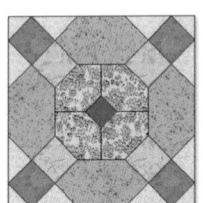
Farmers' Fields

One of North Dakota's biggest economic assets is the **Farmers' Fields** where much of the U.S. spring wheat and rye is grown. The quilt pattern is from the *Kansas City Star* in 1939. North Dakota's state flower is the Wild Prairie Rose. Piecers could try **Prairie Flower** (a) from the Alice Brooks/Laura Wheeler syndicate, or **Prairie Flower** (b), probably from Nancy Cabot.

Bismarck | Dakota Star | Indian Trails

Prairie Star | Lewis and Clark | Washington's Elm

Prairie Flower (a) | Prairie Flower (b) | Tree

North Dakota's state tree is the American elm. So you might piece a **Washington's Elm** from a 1932 *Needlecraft* magazine. A similar block, named simply **Tree**, came from the *Dakota Farmer*, one of many regional farm newspapers that printed patterns submitted by readers. In 1927, Mrs. R.T.P. of Stanley County, North Dakota, sent the design with its simple name. We imagine Mrs. R.T.P. was a Dakota pioneer who pieced quilts in the long winters. For her and the other Dakota quilters, include **Prairie Queen**, a pattern first recorded in Ruth Finley's 1929 book, *Old Patchwork Quilts and the Women Who Made Them*.

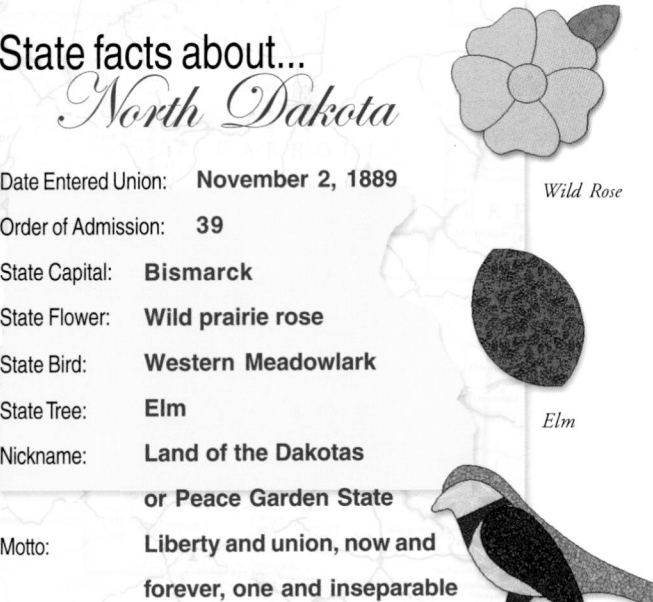

State facts about...
North Dakota

Date Entered Union:	**November 2, 1889**
Order of Admission:	**39**
State Capital:	**Bismarck**
State Flower:	**Wild prairie rose**
State Bird:	**Western Meadowlark**
State Tree:	**Elm**
Nickname:	**Land of the Dakotas or Peace Garden State**
Motto:	**Liberty and union, now and forever, one and inseparable**

Wild Rose

Elm

Meadowlark

Ohio

The State of Ohio was named after the river running along
its southern border. The word Ohio comes from an Indian word
meaning "great" or "beautiful" – descriptions which still apply
to the river, the state and its quilt traditions.

Ohio Beauty appeared in the *Country Home* magazine in May, 1928. *Hearth and Home* magazine's state pattern series from the early twentieth century featured **Ohio**, an unusual pattern later called Ohio Star in *Capper's Weekly* newspaper and State of Ohio in the *Household Magazine* in the '30s. The leaves, resembling buckeye leaves, can be set singly or

Unknown woman in Cincinnati, about 1865.

in groups of four as shown. An Ohio-born reader of the *Kansas City Star* submitted **The Pride of Ohio** for publication in 1939.

The classic **Ohio Star** is pictured in Carrie Hall's 1935 book, *The Romance of the Patchwork Quilt in America*. In her book, Hall states that the star (known by many other names) must be white with a colored background to qualify as an Ohio Star. It's a mystery where Hall found the name and coloring

Ohio Star

advice. Most of her patterns came from earlier sources. It may be that she found the design in the *Ohio Farmer* magazine, which printed the star (dark star on light ground) on October 29, 1896, but gave it no name.

Ohio Beauty   Ohio   Pride of Ohio

Buckeye   Buckeye Beauty (a)   Buckeye Beauty (b)

Ohio Trail   Columbus   Cleveland Lilies

The state tree is the buckeye, known also as the horse chestnut. Ohio may have been nicknamed for that tree. But a more romantic story is that the first territorial governor was called Big Buckeye by the Indians, because he reminded them of a buck deer. The nickname was soon also applied to the territory and later the state. Whichever story is true, everyone now knows Ohio as the Buckeye State. A quilt pattern named **Buckeye** was shown in a 1930s pamphlet from Aunt Martha's Studios. **Buckeye Beauty** (a) is from

Clara Stone's 1906 *Practical Needlework* pamphlet. It is quite similar to a pattern *Farm Journal* calls Road to the White House. This block is perfect for an Ohio quilt, since the state prides itself on the seven Ohio sons elected to the presidency of the United States – a greater number than any other state. So perhaps the road to the White House does run through Ohio.

Ohio Trail is a Nancy Cabot design. The *Progressive Farmer*/Nancy Cabot syndicate published another **Buckeye Beauty** (b) in 1933. This is an older Ladies Art Company pattern called Rockingham's Beauty, but it is easy to see how the name might have been adapted by some Ohio quiltmakers.

Ohio's state capital is Columbus. *Hearth and Home* showed a **Columbus** pattern in their state capital series. This pattern was also called Cleveland Tulips by the *Household Journal* in the '20s. **Cleveland Lilies** is a similar Ladies Art Company pattern. These Cleveland patterns may have been named after Grover Cleveland, President in the 1890s, but they also represent Ohio's largest city.

In the O, the Indian Profile Rock near East Liverpool. In the H, the Ohio River. In the I, the Terminal Tower in Cleveland. In the last O, Union Terminal, Cincinnati.

Scarlet Carnation

Buckeye

Cardinal

State facts about... *Ohio*

Date Entered Union:	**March 1, 1803**
Order of Admission:	**17**
State Capital:	**Columbus**
State Flower:	**Scarlet carnation**
State Bird:	**Cardinal**
State Tree:	**Buckeye**
Nickname:	**Buckeye State**
Motto:	**With God, all things are possible**

Oklahoma

by Patti Butcher, Lawrence, Kansas, 2001.
Machine-pieced and appliquéd by Patti; machine-quilted by Pamela Mayfield.
Patti designed her own quilt, restructuring the vine, and using a large center block surrounded
by small blocks. Patti also redesigned her Oklahoma Sunburst block. The block
in the program and book is the old, traditional Oklahoma Sunburst.

Oklahoma

Sooner State

Oklahoma, the forty-sixth star on our flag, went through the transition from territory to statehood at a time when many ladies' and farm magazines carried quilt patterns. So the state's recent history has been well recorded in quilt design.

One of the earliest patterns is **Oklahoma Boomer**, sold by the Ladies Art Company of St. Louis. It appeared in their early 1890s catalogs, but was dropped from later editions. Oklahoma Boomers ignored settlement laws when Oklahoma was Indian Territory. Boomers squatted in areas closed to whites. In 1889, Congress gave in to the land hunger and sponsored a race for the Indian reserves. Sooners were settlers who jumped the gun on the land run, a part of state history recalled in the nickname, the Sooner State. We can recall the Sooner days with **Road to Oklahoma**, also from the Ladies Art Company catalog.

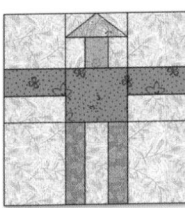

Oklahoma Boomer

Indian Star can honor the native tribes and all the displaced Indians who were moved to the territory in the nineteenth century. The pattern is a variation of the Road to Oklahoma, and appeared in the *Weekly Kansas City Star* in 1937. The state's name comes from the Choctaw language.

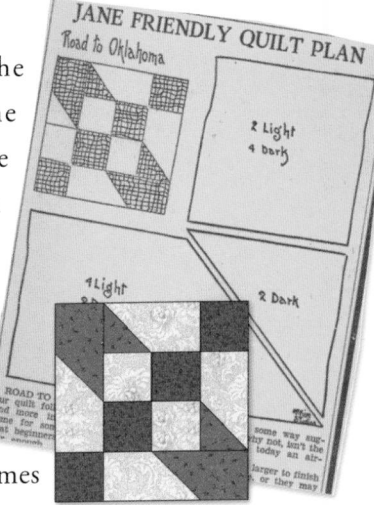

Road to Oklahoma

117

Ukla huma are words for person and red; thus the territory is the home of the Native Americans.

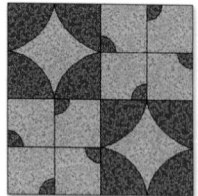

New State

Oklahoma was admitted to the Union in 1907. Three years later, the quilt block, **New State**, was sent to *American Woman* magazine by N.B.L. of Guthrie, Oklahoma. Although she didn't say so, we can be confident that N.B.L. was honoring her home state. Around that time, *Hearth and Home* magazine asked its readers to contribute pieced blocks for each state. **Oklahoma**

Oklahoma

was chosen for the Sooner State. In the teens the magazine's readers sent in blocks for each state capital, with **Guthrie** representing the original capital of Oklahoma. Although Oklahoma City had succeeded Guthrie as the state capital in 1910, it apparently had not taken its place in the hearts of *Hearth and Home* readers.

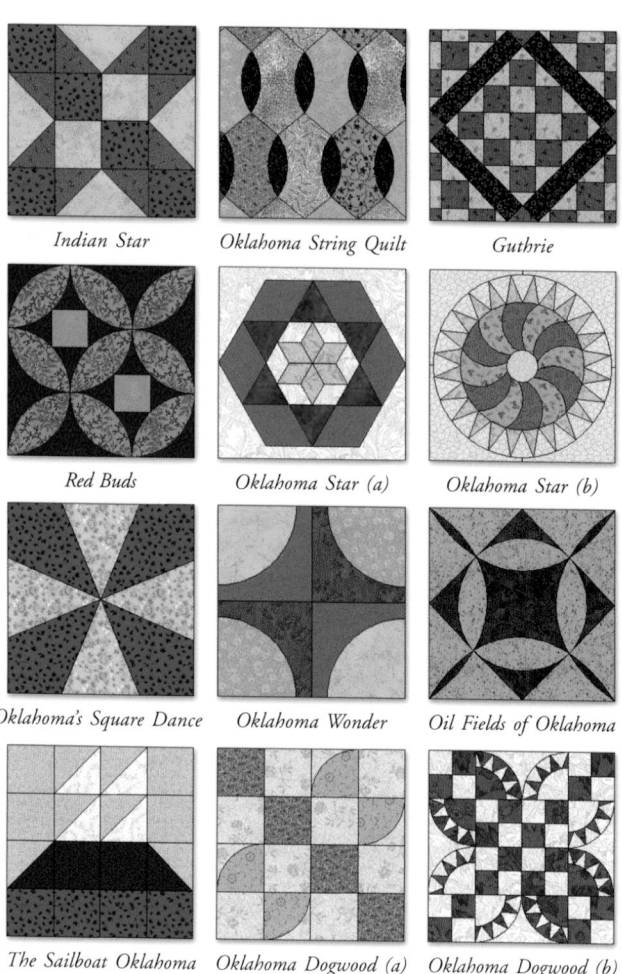

Indian Star   *Oklahoma String Quilt*   *Guthrie*

Red Buds   *Oklahoma Star (a)*   *Oklahoma Star (b)*

Oklahoma's Square Dance   *Oklahoma Wonder*   *Oil Fields of Oklahoma*

The Sailboat Oklahoma   *Oklahoma Dogwood (a)*   *Oklahoma Dogwood (b)*

IMPATIENT FOR HIS PROMISED STATEHOOD.

In this cartoon by Albert Reid for Capper's Mail and Breeze, Oklahoma is an impatient cowboy courting the coquettish Republicans. "I'm tired of being put off." Courtesy of the Kansas Center for Historical Research.

Ardmore, Oklahoma, has a block to commemorate it. **The Ardmore**, a winner in a fourth graders' block contest, appeared in the *Oklahoma Farmer Stockman's* 1932 *Good Cheer*

The Ardmore

quilt pattern column. This column ran in the '20s and '30s, offering reader-contributed patterns, a typical method of pattern exchange in regional farm periodicals of the time.

During the same era, the *Weekly Kansas City Star* ran a similar, but much more extensive, quilt column in

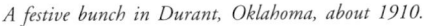

A festive bunch in Durant, Oklahoma, about 1910.

"Our home at Gale, Oklahoma, 1914, George, Allie and Ione."

Pond Creek, Oklahoma, 1914.

their farm newspaper, which had a special Texas/ Oklahoma edition. Thus there were many Oklahoma contributions to the *Kansas City Star* series. **Oklahoma Star** (a) appeared in 1945. **Oklahoma**

Oklahoma Sunburst

Sunburst, a new name for an old pattern, was given in 1933. **Oklahoma's Square Dance** was shown in 1957. **The Oil Fields of Oklahoma** honored the state's principal resource in 1940. And in 1944, during World War II, a *Kansas City Star* reader memorialized a navy ship with **The Sailboat Oklahoma**. **Oklahoma String Quilt** isn't really a string quilt, pieced of narrow "strings" of fabric, but that's the name that appeared in the *Star* in 1950. And **Oklahoma Wonder** is a 1956 *Star* contribution.

Marilyn Lithgow christened an old pattern **Oklahoma Star** (b) in her 1974 book, *Quiltmaking and Quiltmakers*. **Oklahoma Dogwood** (a&b), sold in the Mountain Mist series, requires two blocks alternated.

(The sawtooth block in this design was also shown as Dogwood Blossom in a 1928 issue of *Capper's Weekly*.) Dogwoods, like redbuds, are an early sign of Oklahoma spring. As the Oklahoma state tree, the redbud is commemorated by a pieced **Red Buds**, an allover pattern based on circles and squares from a 1930s Nancy Cabot column in the *Chicago Tribune*.

Mistletoe

Redbud

Scissor-Tailed Flycatcher

State facts about...
Oklahoma

Date Entered Union:	**November 16, 1907**
Order of Admission:	**46**
State Capital:	**Oklahoma City**
State Flower:	**Mistletoe**
State Bird:	**Scissor-tailed flycatcher**
State Tree:	**Redbud**
Nickname:	**Sooner State**
Motto:	***Labor omnia vincit***
	(Labor conquers all things)

Oregon
Beaver State

In 1841, 30 men, women, and children set out for Oregon country
from Independence, Missouri, the edge of the United States.
They were the first of thousands of emigrants to cross the Oregon Trail,
inspired by promises of land and gold.

The origins of the name Oregon are mysterious. Early maps of western America showed an imaginary river flowing to the Pacific through a deep pass in the Rocky Mountains, creating a valley that explorers hoped would be the fabled Northwest Passage. The mythical river was labeled the Ovaricon; one variation of the word became Wisconsin (explorers first hoped that midwestern river flowed all the way to the Pacific) and another was Oregon, a melodious name that was first applied to the whole northwestern corner of the American continent, and later to the state.

Oregon is a pattern sent by Mrs. N.S. of Mayville, Oregon, to *Hearth and Home* magazine about 1910, when readers were asked to submit patterns named for their states. **Oregon Trail** is one of many names for a popular pattern, usually pieced of two contrasting shades. Carlie Sexton, who wrote about quilts in the late 1920s, showed Oregon Trail as a three-color block.

Oregon

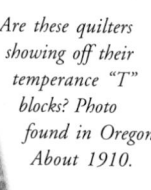

Are these quilters showing off their temperance "T" blocks? Photo found in Oregon. About 1910.

Like most quilt block names, we have no idea how long quiltmakers have called the design Oregon Trail. But it's unlikely that the women who walked the trail, and rode the wagons, actually made Oregon Trail quilts. Most of these quilts date from after 1880, when the railroads were carrying people west. In fact, while on the trail, women seemed to have made few quilts.

Oregon Trail	*Lewis and Clark*	*Fifty-Four Forty or Fight*
Duck's Foot in the Mud	*Grape Vines*	*Grape Basket*
Tree of Paradise	*Columbia Puzzle*	*Salem*

Wagon Tracks

A comprehensive collection of their diaries, gathered by Kenneth L. Holmes in the series *Covered Wagon Women*, includes few references to sewing. The grueling trips, with the roughness of the ride, left women exhausted each evening. We can remember the covered-wagon women with **Wagon Tracks**, the block representing Oregon in Ruby Short McKim's 1930s syndicated newspaper column, *Patchwork Parade of States*.

The Americans who settled Oregon in the 1840s brought a long-simmering dispute between Britain and the United States to a boil. The Oregon country was claimed as U.S. territory by Lewis and Clark in the first years of the nineteenth century. Recall Oregon history with **Lewis and Clark** from Clara Stone's 1906 quilt pattern pamphlet. England laid claim to the same land. The countries could not agree on an east/west line dividing the United States and Canada. By 1846 it was a political issue. Americans demanded a border at the 54.40 point of latitude, far into what is now Canadian territory. "Fifty-Four Forty or Fight," was a political slogan of expansionist President James K. Polk's supporters. A compromise defined the border at 49 degrees, where it remains. **Fifty-Four Forty or Fight** also became a quilt pattern. The name was recorded decades later by Ruth Finley in her 1929 book, *Old Patchwork Quilts and the Women Who Made Them*.

Herding sheep, postcard mailed in 1916.

The message: "There is a box of cherries on the train today." 1912.

"Illuminated tunnel, near Bonneville Dam, Columbia River Highway, Oregon."

"Seining Salmon Near the Dalles, Oregon."

"Portland and Mt. Hood by Moonlight. A sight equal to this but few cities have to offer. Particularly at night-time, on account of atmospheric conditions, the snow-capped Mt. Hood stands out clearly in the distance."

The Oregon Territory became a state in 1859. Its capital is **Salem**, commemorated with a block from *Hearth and Home*. Oregonians call their state the Beaver State or Webfoot State; represent the latter nickname with **Duck's Foot in the Mud** from Ruth Finley's 1929 quilt book.

The state's official flower is the Oregon Grape. Nancy Cabot offered a **Grape Vines** pattern. To hold the grapes, consider **Grape Basket**, from the Ladies Art Company catalog. The state tree is the Douglas Fir; I could not find a fir pattern, but the **Tree of Paradise** from *Farm Journal* in 1925 can remind us how welcome Oregon's forests must have been to the women who had crossed the western deserts.

For the last days of the trip the travelers kept their eyes on Mt. Hood, the highest point in the Cascade Mountain Range. Recall snow-covered Mt. Hood with an old block known by two appropriate names. The block appeared as **The Mountain Peak** in a 1943 *Kansas City Star* column. It was also called Snowflake in the 1890's Ladies Art Company catalog. Another of Oregon's scenic and economic assets is the Columbia River, symbolized with **Columbia Puzzle**, also from the Ladies Art Company.

The Mountain Peak

State facts about...
Oregon

Date Entered Union:	**February 14, 1859**
Order of Admission:	**33**
State Capital:	**Salem**
State Flower:	**Oregon grape**
State Bird:	**Western meadowlark**
State Tree:	**Douglas fir**
Nickname:	**Beaver State, Webfoot State**
Motto:	***Alis volat propriis***
	(She flies with her own wings)

Grape

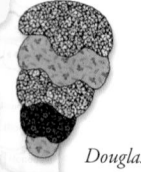

Douglas Fir

Western Meadowlark

122

Pennsylvania

Keystone State

Pennsylvania has much history to be proud of – including its traditions
as a birthplace of American freedoms and as a home of outstanding quilt design
and craftsmanship. Pennsylvania's Amish quilts are world famous, as are its red
and green appliqués based on Pennsylvania German design traditions.

Pennsylvania (a) is the block that represented the state in *Hearth and Home* magazine's early twentieth-century series of state blocks. *Workbasket* magazine also ran a state block series, in which **Pennsylvania Pineapple** represented the Keystone State. The Nancy Page syndicated column called a double Nine-Patch **Pennsylvania** (b).

Pennsylvania Pineapple

The Pennsylvania Germans, often called the Pennsylvania Dutch (Pennsylvania Deutsch) have contributed much to American design. The Germanic tradition is apparent in the eight-lobed rosettes and three-lobed tulips, such as the flower in **Pennsylvania Tulip** from Mountain Mist patterns. Potted flowers, pomegranates, the Basque cross (similar to a swastika), and the heart are other design ideas descended from traditional German ornament. Writers looking at folk art in the twentieth century also saw connections between hexagonal

Pennsylvania Tulip

stars and Pennsylvania Dutch hex signs that adorn barns in southern Pennsylvania. *Hearth and Home's* **Pennsylvania Wheel Quilt** reflects the barn ornament.

The capital of Pennsylvania is **Harrisburg**, a pattern from *Hearth and Home's* state capital series. For many years, Philadelphia was the largest and most cosmopolitan city in the United States. Laid out by master planner William Penn, the city's impressive and orderly grid of streets were named not after kings,

Penn's Puzzle

princes or politicians, but in Quaker fashion (exalting no man above another), after trees and numbers. All of us who live today on Spruce or Chestnut, with no spruce or chestnut tree in sight, owe the mystery of the missing tree to Penn, an American tradition we can commemorate with **Penn's Puzzle** from Nancy Cabot.

Philadelphia Patch

Philadelphia's orderly streets are reflected in Carlie Sexton's **Philadelphia Pavement** (a), from her 1928 catalog, *Old Fashioned Quilts*. Ruth Finley, in her book *Old Patchwork Quilts and the Women Who Made Them*, showed another neat **Philadelphia Pavement** (b). But the Ladies Art Company's **Philadelphia Patch** seems unrelated to the city plan. It is numbered

 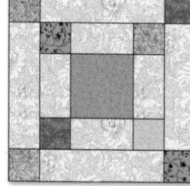 

Pennsylvania (a)   *Pennsylvania (b)*   *Allentown*

Independence Square   *Laurel Wreath*   *Harrisburg*

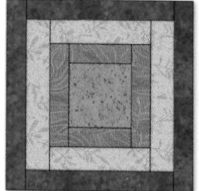  

Philadelphia   *Philadelphia*   *Pennsylvania Wheel*
Pavement (a)   *Pavement (b)*   *Quilt*

492 in their catalog, indicating that it was not in the original 1898 publication, which contains lower numbers, but was a twentieth-century addition. **Allentown** is another Pennsylvania city with its own quilt block, again from Nancy Page.

Pennsylvania's history, and geography as well, have inspired several pattern names. Originally founded by William Penn, the colony was to be named New Wales, because of the hilly landscape. But English rulers frowned on that choice. Penn then decided to name it Sylvania, which means woods. King Charles II of England changed the name to Pennsylvania, a joke and insult to Penn, who believed a colony named for an individual to be a vanity.

Settlement of the colony, as with most American territory, was not without conflict between the

A couple photographed in Reading about 1890.

Downtown Philadelphia from a Druco-Optus Drug Store, postcard.

"Valley Forge lies 24 miles from Philadelphia on the banks of the Schuylkill River where the picturesque Valley Creek empties into it. Washington's Army laid encamped on these hills from Dec. 19, 1777, until June 19, 1778."

settlers and the Native Americans. The local Ottawa Indians were led in an unsuccessful uprising against the British by Chief Pontiac in 1763. A **Pontiac Star**,

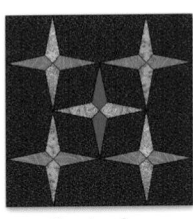

Pontiac Star

from Clara Stone's 1906 *Practical Needlework* catalog, symbolizes the original Pennsylvanians. Later, the colonists began their own, more successful, uprising against the British, making Philadelphia the Revolution's center. There the Declaration of Independence was signed. The Famous Features syndicate included **Independence Square** in their 1976 bicentennial quilts catalog to commemorate the historic site. Of course, the colors suggested for the block were red, white, and blue.

Valley Forge Quilt

Valley Forge, where the colonial army spent a harsh winter, is another site made famous during Revolutionary times. A 1941 issue of *Country Gentleman* magazine pictured a quilt supposedly used on General George Washington's bed in that camp. The pattern is known as the **Valley Forge Quilt** or the George Washington

Quilt. A lesser-known battle is the Wyoming Valley Massacre, which took place near what is now Wilkes-Barre. A group of colonists was killed by British soldiers and Indians in their pay. The Nancy Cabot/*Progressive Farmer* syndicate had a **Wyoming Valley Block** quilt, possibly named for this part of Pennsylvania.

Wyoming Valley Block

Benjamin Franklin, statesman, philosopher, and inventor, is a Pennsylvania native son. **The Tail of Benjamin's Kite** commemorates his electrical exploration with a kite and key. 1920s quilt

The Tail of Benjamin's Kite

historian, Ruth Finley, says this is a regional name in Pennsylvania for the three-color variation of a block known elsewhere as Jacob's Ladder.

The state flower is the Mountain Laurel. *Capper's Weekly* included a pieced **Laurel Wreath** in a 1930s pamphlet, *Quilting: A New, Old Art*.

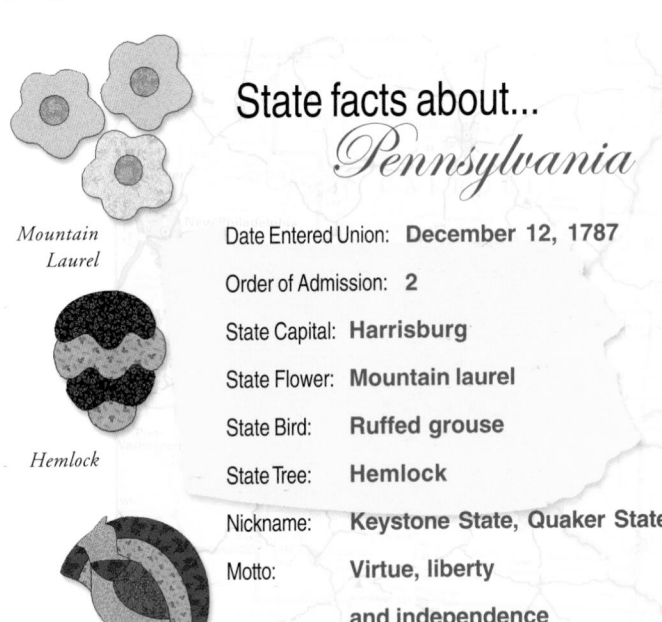

Mountain Laurel

Hemlock

Ruffed Grouse

State facts about... *Pennsylvania*

Date Entered Union:	**December 12, 1787**
Order of Admission:	**2**
State Capital:	**Harrisburg**
State Flower:	**Mountain laurel**
State Bird:	**Ruffed grouse**
State Tree:	**Hemlock**
Nickname:	**Keystone State, Quaker State**
Motto:	**Virtue, liberty and independence**

125

Rhode Island

Ocean State

Rhode Island, the first colony to declare its independence
from Great Britain, and the last of the original 13 to ratify the Constitution,
celebrated 200 years of statehood in 1990.

Five hundred years ago the first European explorers found Indians from the Algonquin tribes living in the area. To represent the Native Americans, include the block **Algonquin Charm** from the *Chicago Tribune's* 1930's Nancy Cabot quilt pattern column.

Dutch explorers named the Narragansett Bay islands Roodt Eylandt, or Red Island, for their red clay shores. The first European settlers, banished from the

Rhode Island

Massachusetts Bay Colony for religious dissension, founded small colonies in Providence and other towns. These towns were united in 1647 under the name Rhode Island and Providence Plantations. So our smallest state was also the first state named. Remember the state with the **Rhode Island** block submitted about 1910 to *Hearth and Home* magazine's state block series by a Tiverton reader who called herself Patience Pettigrew.

Providence has been the sole capital since 1900 (before that the state had multiple capitals). *Hearth and Home* published a block called **Providence**, which was adapted and renamed **Providence Star** by *Workbasket* magazine for their 1935 All-States Quilt.

Providence

Rhode Island's early prosperity was due to the shipping industry. Recall the clipper ships with a **Mariner's Compass**, this one from a 1931 article by Ruth Finley in *Country Gentleman* magazine. The coast remains important to the state's economy; its nickname is the Ocean State. **Ocean Wave** (a) can stand for the beautiful shoreline. This popular pattern

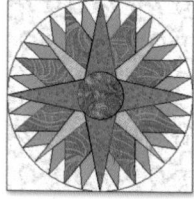

Mariner's Compass

appeared in many variations, including perhaps the first named **Ocean Wave** (b), published by the *Ohio Farmer* magazine in 1894. The Ladies Art Company called an all-over triangle design **Ocean Waves** at about the same time. Another design to represent the coast is **Clamshell**, which Ruby McKim used for Rhode Island in her 1930s *Patchwork Parade of States* series.

Spinning Jenny

Rhode Island became an innovator in textile production when America's first power cotton spinning machines, called Spinning Jennies, were built in Pawtucket by Samuel Slater about the time of the Revolutionary War. Remember Slater's Mill, which led to abundant American calico and our classic calico quilts, with **Spinning Jenny** from the Nancy Cabot column.

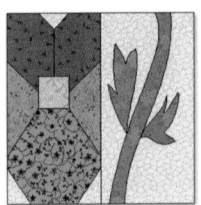
Johnny Jump-Up

Rhode Island's state flower is the violet or the Johnny Jump-up. *Woman's World* magazine printed **Johnny Jump-up** in 1933. The block is an unusual design, forming an all over pattern of flowers on stems when staggered blocks are sewn together. The Nancy Cabot column renamed an older design **Violet Blossoms** at about the same time.

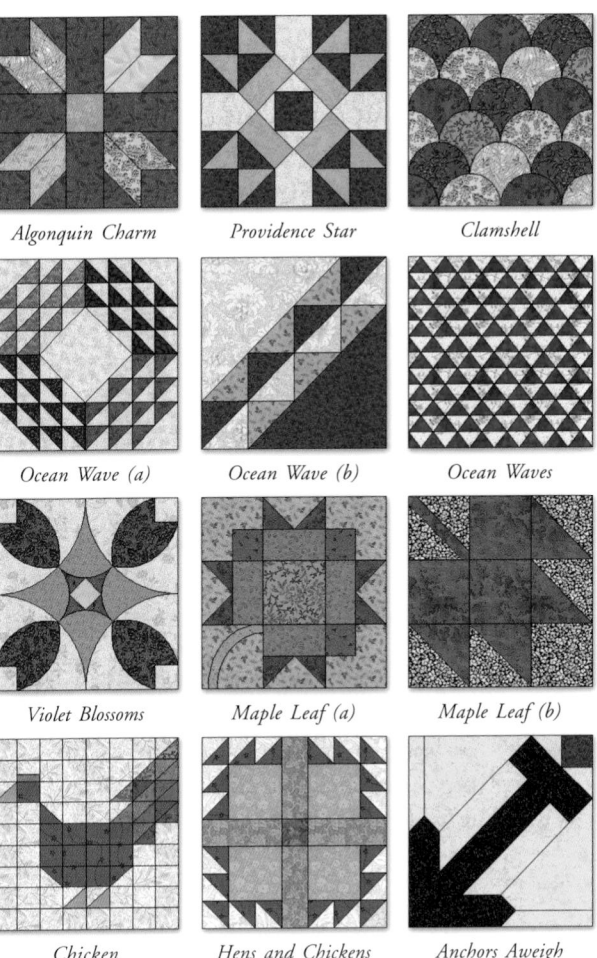

Algonquin Charm   *Providence Star*   *Clamshell*

Ocean Wave (a)   *Ocean Wave (b)*   *Ocean Waves*

Violet Blossoms   *Maple Leaf (a)*   *Maple Leaf (b)*

Chicken   *Hens and Chickens*   *Anchors Aweigh*

The Red Maple is the state tree. Represent this tree in shades of red with **Maple Leaf** (a) from Aunt Martha Studios in the '30s, and **Maple Leaf** (b) from Clara Stone's 1906 *Practical Needlework* pamphlet.

"Little Rhody's" state bird is the Rhode Island Red. *Needlecraft* magazine designed a pieced **Chicken** block of triangles and squares in 1928. Or you might prefer a symbolic representation: **Hens and Chickens** is from the Ladies Art Company catalog of quilt patterns around the late 1890s.

The state's motto is "Hope," represented by an anchor on the state seal and flag. Nineteenth-century quiltmakers occasionally included appliquéd anchors in their album quilts to represent this virtue. For a pieced block, include **Anchors Aweigh** from the Laura Wheeler/Alice Brooks column during World War II.

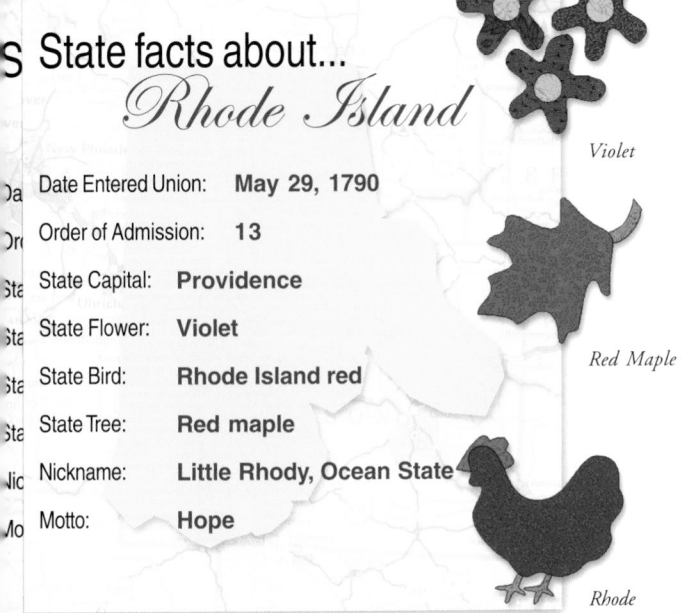

State facts about...
Rhode Island

Violet

Date Entered Union:	**May 29, 1790**
Order of Admission:	**13**
State Capital:	**Providence**
State Flower:	**Violet**
State Bird:	**Rhode Island red**
State Tree:	**Red maple**
Nickname:	**Little Rhody, Ocean State**
Motto:	**Hope**

Red Maple

Rhode Island Red

South Dakota

Sunshine State

South Dakota is the lower half of the Dakota Territory created in 1861.
By the time the residents were ready for statehood, two distinct settled areas
had grown up. So two states entered the Union in 1889.

The Dakota Territory's first settlers were the Indians, among them the tribe we call Sioux, but who called themselves Lakota or Dakota, meaning "friends" or "allied tribes." Symbolize the geography, and the first people, with **Prairie Star**. Carrie Hall recorded this name in her 1935 book, *The Romance of the Patchwork Quilt in America*. The design, an old favorite, is a star favored by the Sioux Indians, who are productive quiltmakers today. This makes it especially appropriate for the Dakotas.

Hearth and Home magazine's series of state-named designs included **South Dakota**. A few years later the magazine printed **Pierre**, a feathered star, for the state capital. And at some time in the early twentieth century *Hearth and Home* printed **Dakota Star**, a pattern for the Dakotas to share.

"Phillips Ave., looking South, Sioux Falls, S.D."

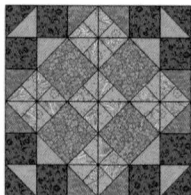

South Dakota

130

Emma B. Avery and family, South Dakota, 1915.

Prairie Star — *Pierre* — *Dakota Star*

Gold Brick — *Rising Sun (a)* — *Rising Sun (b)*

Pine Tree — *Tree of Paradise* — *Sunshiny Day*

The Dakotas were settled in the last half of the nineteenth century by immigrants from Europe and the eastern U.S. looking for land to homestead. Immigration boomed when gold was discovered in the South Dakota's Black Hills. **Gold Brick** from the Aunt Martha Studios can symbolize the boom town era and South Dakota's continuing gold production. The quilt pattern is from the *Kansas City Star* in 1939.

South Dakota calls itself the Sunshine State. To remember the nickname make **Sunshiny Day**, a

Farm Journal design. The Dakota Farmer printed two versions of **Rising Sun** (a&b).

The state tree, the Black Hills spruce, could be represented by any of many pieced evergreens such as **Pine Tree** from the *Kansas City Star* in 1934 or **Tree of Paradise** from *Farm Journal*. Because North and South Dakota share much history and geography, you'll want to check the North Dakota patterns too.

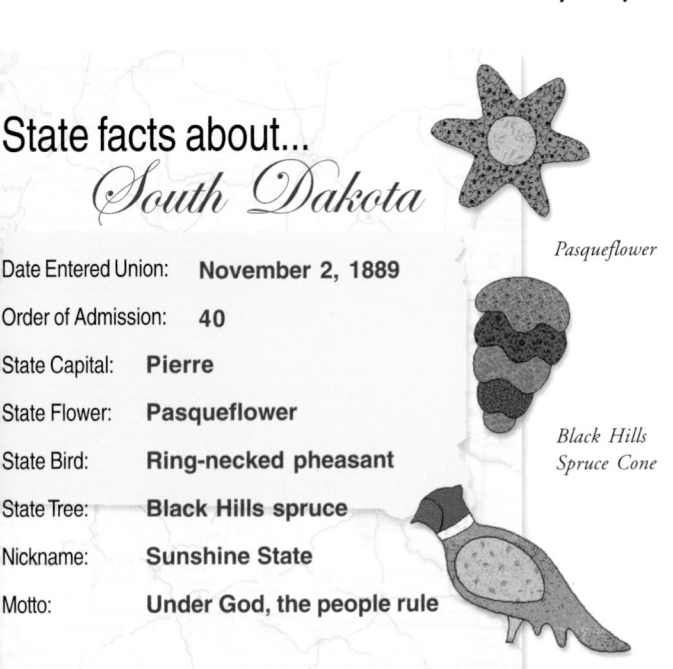

State facts about...
South Dakota

Date Entered Union:	**November 2, 1889**
Order of Admission:	**40**
State Capital:	**Pierre**
State Flower:	**Pasqueflower**
State Bird:	**Ring-necked pheasant**
State Tree:	**Black Hills spruce**
Nickname:	**Sunshine State**
Motto:	**Under God, the people rule**

Pasqueflower

Black Hills Spruce Cone

Ring-necked Pheasant

Esther sent this postcard from the Black Hills in 1953.

Tennessee

Volunteer State

Like so many lyrical state names, Tennessee comes
from a Native American language. Tanasi or Tinnase was a Cherokee village
along the Little Tennessee River. This name was also given, much later,
to several quilt blocks.

The Nancy Page quilt column in the 1930s named a simple pattern **Tennessee** (a) after the sixteenth state. A reader of *Hearth and Home* magazine in the early twentieth century contributed a striped star and called it **Tennessee** (b).

Tennessee Snowball

One popular pattern has at least sixteen names, including **Tennessee Snowball**, a name given to it by *Woman's World* magazine, circa 1930. The *Prairie Farmer* magazine featured **Tennessee Circles**, which makes an intricate design when set all over.

Nashville is Tennessee's capital. Around 1910, *Hearth and Home* conducted a contest for state capital quilt blocks, and a reader came up with a **Nashville** block for "the Athens of the South." Another town, Cumberland Gap, is much smaller, and lies near the

Nashville

passage through the Appalachian Mountains. Nancy Cabot designed a unique **Cumberland Gap** pattern which does look like a mountain pass.

Daniel Boone traveled through the Cumberland Gap, blazing a trail to Tennessee and the wilderness

Daniel Boone Quilt

beyond. Betty Flack published the **Daniel Boone Quilt**, which she adapted from a quilt she saw in an old photo of Daniel Boone's fort. The medallion pattern appeared in her *ABC Publications* in July, 1964.

Davy Crockett is another Tennessee pioneer, born in the "Volunteer State." Martha Marshall in *Quilts of Appalachia* shows a quilt pattern she calls the **Crockett Cabin Quilt**, because she saw one in Crockett's birthplace in Jonesboro. In honor of "Old Hickory,"

Crockett Cabin Quilt

Andrew Jackson, an American president from Tennessee, we include a **Jackson Star**, named by Eveline Foland in a 1931 *Kansas City Star*.

Tennessee (a)

Tennessee (b)

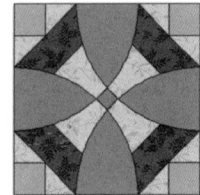
Tennessee Circles

Jackson Star

Iris Leaf

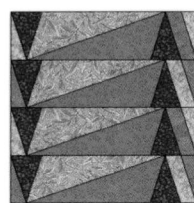
Cumberland Gap

Tennessee's state flower is the iris. Commemorate it by stitching up a modernistic **Pieced Iris** from Ruby McKim. Or include a pieced **Iris Leaf**, which Eveline Foland noted was always green on white. In any other colors it was commonly known as Turkey Tracks or Wandering Foot.

Pieced Iris

"Henley Street Bridge is recognized as one of the most beautiful structures of its kind in the entire south. It is on the main highway leading to the Great Smoky Mountains National Park and is named in honor of Colonel David Henley, a Revolutionary Soldier."

State facts about...
Tennessee

Date Entered Union:	**June 1, 1796**
Order of Admission:	**16**
State Capital:	**Nashville**
State Flower:	**Iris**
State Bird:	**Mockingbird**
State Tree:	**Tulip tree**
Nickname:	**Volunteer State**
Motto:	**Agriculture and commerce**

Iris

Tulip Tree

Mockingbird

Texas
Lone Star State

Texas is a land of superlatives. Inevitably, the state holds
the record for patterns named in its honor. The state's name, which fits it so well,
was a happy accident – the result of intercultural confusion.

Sixteenth-century Spanish explorers had heard of a great kingdom of Texas, so they gave the territory that name. One hundred years later, their followers realized that the word Techas was a greeting in a native language, not the name of a tribe or a place. But what better name for a state that prides itself on its hospitality?

_Unknown woman, Texas,
about 1875._

After breaking away from Mexico, Texas became an independent republic. The sovereign state's flag flourished a single star, the origin of the nickname the Lone Star State. The Lone Star is also the pattern name given a bed-sized quilt with an eight-pointed star pieced of diamonds. One Texas mystery is the source of this pattern name. When I wrote an article on Texas patterns for _Quilters Newsletter Magazine_ in 1981, I thought that the Ladies Art Company had included this pattern in their original catalog of the 1890s. But I later figured out (thanks to other pattern historians, Cuesta Benberry and Wilene Smith), that the pattern was a twentieth-century addition. Both Carlie Sexton and Ruby McKim, in her _Patchwork Parade of States_, printed the name Lone Star in the

Lone Star (a) Lone Star (b) Crossroads to Texas

Texas (a) Texas (b) Texas (c)

The Star of Alamo Texas Tears (a) Texas Tears (b)

1965. And to confuse us further, the Laura Wheeler column syndicated two other **Lone Stars** (a&b) in the 1930s.

Many other Texas patterns use the star motif. *Hearth and Home* magazine's state block series, in the early 1900s, featured a five-pointed **Texas** (a) star with the letters T-E-X-A-S in the points.

Austin

Ruth Finley showed a Nine-Patch star variation she called **Texas** (b) in her 1929 book *Old Patchwork Quilts and the Women Who Made Them*. A similar star, named for **Austin**, was submitted when *Hearth and Home* magazine asked readers for patterns named for state capitals. Nancy Page's 1930s quilt column gave the name **Texas** (c) to a star pattern better known as Fifty-Four Forty or Fight. Aunt Martha's Studio, from Kansas City, also sold a **Texas Star** – this one six-pointed.

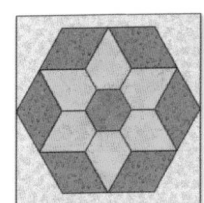

Texas Star

early 1930s. So one of them was probably the first to publish the name Lone Star for the whole-top design. But I haven't yet figured out which. The Home Art Company called it Pride of Texas soon after.

The Lone Star

The Lone Star quilt design is far older than that published name. The earliest dated quilt I've seen with this star design is inscribed 1835. I guess that in the nineteenth century the pattern was called Rising Sun, or Star of Bethlehem. I found an old clipping of a block-size star of diamonds named **The Lone Star** dated 1915, but I don't know the pattern source. This may be the origin of the name for the medallion pattern too. We can sum up this question with **Texas Puzzle** from *Aunt Kate's Quilting Bee* in

Texas Puzzle

Cowboy Star by Jean Stanclift, Lawrence, Kansas, 1998.

"Dallas, City of Opportunity," 1945.

Texas Pointer

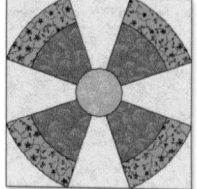
Texas Tulip

Texas Rose

Texas Treasure

Texas Trellis

Texas Cactus Basket

Texas Daisy

Texas Sunflower (a)

Texas Sunflower (b)

Texas Ranger

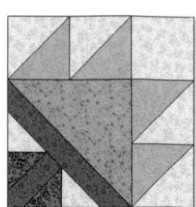
Texas Flower

named after the Texas fort. Finley attributes the name **Texas Tears** (a) to this bloody time in Texas history. A second **Texas Tears** (b) block is from the Ladies Art Company. The *American Woman* magazine remembered the **Texas Ranger**, who provided law and order as Texas was settled. **Texas Pointer** is from the *Kansas City Star* in 1934.

There are several Texas florals. Ladies Art Company offered a **Texas Flower**. **Texas Tulip** is from Nancy Cabot. And a **Texas Rose** or Texas Treasure is from Ruth Finley. Another **Texas Treasure** pattern comes from Nancy Page. And the *Kansas City Star* printed **Texas Trellis** in 1943 for all these flowers to climb. Della Harris, a small pattern company from Waco, designed a **Texas Daisy** in the 1930s. *Comfort* magazine had a **Texas Sunflower** (a), as did Nancy Cabot (b). Nancy Cabot also syndicated an elaborate pattern she called **Texas Cactus Basket**.

A century earlier, the Texas fight for independence from Mexico certainly inspired a spirit of American patriotism. Immigrants found many **Crossroads to Texas** (a Ladies Art Company pattern) on their way to settle Texas. The struggle for Texas sovereignty resulted in the Battle of the Alamo. **The Star of Alamo** is a 1941 *Kansas City Star* pattern. It was actually named by an Arkansas boy for his school, which was

Unknown woman, Cuero, Texas, about 1875.

Cigar Box label. The cowboy image has been selling tobacco for generations.

Bluebonnet

Pecan

Mockingbird

State facts about... *Texas*

Date Entered Union:	**December 29, 1845**
Order of Admission:	**28**
State Capital:	**Austin**
State Flower:	**Bluebonnet**
State Bird:	**Mockingbird**
State Tree:	**Pecan**
Nickname:	**Lone Star State**
Motto:	**Friendship**

Utah
Beehive State

Like several of the original colonies, Utah is a state founded as a religious colony. Brigham Young and his Mormon followers came west in the 1840s to avoid the religious prejudice they encountered in the eastern states.

Remember the Mormon trail with the **Trail of the Covered Wagon**, a name from Ruth Finley's 1929 book, *Old Patchwork Quilts and the Women Who Made Them.* The pioneers settled in the desert near the Great Salt Lake and named their colony Deseret. We can remember the old name with a **Desert Rose** (a) block, also from Ruth Finley, or another **Desert Rose** (b) from the *Chicago Tribune's* Nancy Cabot column.

Trail of the Covered Wagon

The area that became Utah was also the land of the Utes. So when the federal government named the territory, they chose Utah to remember the Native Americans. We can remember them with **Indian Puzzle**, also from Nancy Cabot, or **Indian Arrowhead**, from the Aunt Martha pattern company.

The block **Utah** was one a reader submitted to *Hearth and Home* magazine's state block pattern series. **Utah Star** is probably from the Nancy Cabot column. **Salt Lake City** was the entry for the state's capital in *Hearth and Home's* capitals' series.

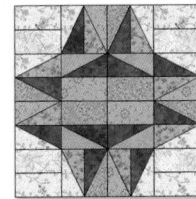

Utah Star

To recall Utah's nickname, the Beehive State, piece a **Honey Bee** from Ruby McKim's syndicated column in the late 1920s. The state flower is the Sego Lily,

Home is where... ♥

by Shauna O. Christensen, Lawrence, Kansas, 2000.
Machine-pieced and appliquéd, and machine-quilted. To honor four different states,
Shauna used birds, flowers, leaves and cones to represent California, Utah, Kansas and Washington.
The Log Cabin blocks in her quilt's center represent home.
Rotating these blocks created a traditional set called Barn Raising.

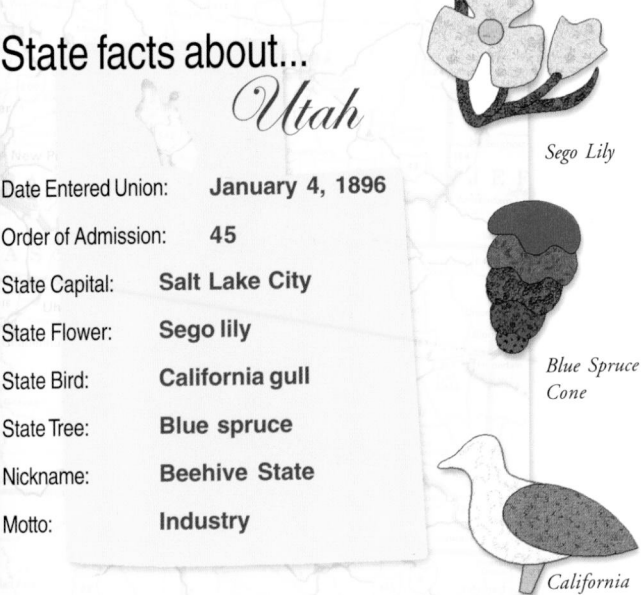

"The first house built in Utah is now the Temple Square in Salt Lake City. Erected in 1847 by the pioneers, this log cabin is preserved as a reminder to present and future generations of the hardships endured by the founders of this commonwealth."

Desert Rose (a)   *Desert Rose (b)*   *Indian Puzzle*

Indian Arrowhead   *Utah*   *Salt Lake City*

Honey Bee   *The Lily*   *Lily*

Tree of Paradise (a)   *Tree of Paradise (b)*   *Flock of Birds*

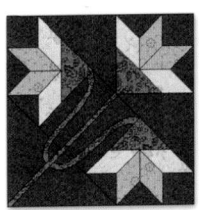

A Lily Quilt

a tri-lobed white bloom. Lilies have long been popular with quilters, so a traditional design like **A Lily Quilt** from the *Orange Judd Farmer* in 1901 or **The Lily** from Carlie Sexton, will represent the flower in a pieced design. A more modern variation is **Lily** designed by the Alice Brooks/Laura Wheeler syndicate in the 1930s.

The state tree is the blue spruce, which can be represented by any of many pieced evergreen tree blocks, such as **Tree of Paradise** (a) from *Woman's World* magazine or another **Tree of Paradise** (b) from *Modern Priscilla* magazine. The state bird is the California Gull, honored for its legendary attack on the grasshopper plague in the early days of the territory. Picture the gulls symbolically in **Birds in the Air**, a variation of the Honeybee design from the Coats and Clark pattern catalog in 1942, or **Flock of Birds** from the syndicated Nancy Page column.

Birds in the Air

State facts about...
Utah

Sego Lily

Blue Spruce Cone

California Gull

Date Entered Union:	**January 4, 1896**
Order of Admission:	**45**
State Capital:	**Salt Lake City**
State Flower:	**Sego lily**
State Bird:	**California gull**
State Tree:	**Blue spruce**
Nickname:	**Beehive State**
Motto:	**Industry**

Vermont

Green Mountain State

Vermont is one of the few American states with a history as an independent republic. Once Algonquin Indian territory, the mountainous country was conquered by the Iroquois, then the French, and the British. Prior to our Revolution, Vermont's colonial neighbors also had designs on the land.

Massachusetts, New Hampshire and New York claimed sovereignty at various times and in various places. The local militia, the Green Mountain Boys, earned a fierce reputation by first expelling the New Yorkers and then the British, establishing a republic in 1777. The country, initially called New Connecticut, adopted a constitution forbidding slavery, becoming the first American government to do so.

Vermont was also the first new state to join the original 13 colonies. After fourteen years of independence, they negotiated a territorial settlement with New York and formed an alliance with the Union. The residents of New Connecticut adopted a new name. "Vermont" recalls the state's French history and the mountain range running through the state. The French words for Green Mountains are Les Monts Verts.

In 1907 the New England magazine *Hearth and Home* asked readers to mail quilt patterns named for the various states. Over the next ten years they printed at least one design for each state and territory and their capitals. **Vermont** (a) represents the Green Mountain State. In the 1930s, the Nancy Page quilt column, which was syndicated to many newspapers throughout the country published both **Vermont** (b) and **Hills of Vermont**. This last block is similar to an old pattern known as Lady of the Lake, so it can also symbolize Lake Champlain on the state's western border.

Hills of Vermont

Green Mountain Star is a name recorded by Clara Stone, a New England pattern source from the early twentieth century. The Green Mountain State also shares the

White Mountains with New Hampshire, so you'll want to include **The Mountain Peak** from a 1943 *Kansas City Star*, a block to recall snowy mountains since it's also known as Snowflake and Snow Block.

The combination of mountain scenery and white-painted villages, with their characteristic church steeples, make Vermont one of America's prettiest places. It is the most rural state, with fewer city dwellers than any of the other fifty states. And only the far larger states of Alaska and Wyoming have fewer inhabitants. In a state of small towns, the state capital remains one more small town. **Montpelier**, named by the French, is remembered in a design from *Hearth and Home*.

Montpelier

When syndicated quilt columnist, Ruby Short McKim, designed her *Patchwork Parade of States* in the early 1930s, she chose a traditional pattern she found from Mrs. Danner's mail order patterns in 1934, and called it **Clover Blossom** for Vermont. Choose a raspberry red shade for the bloom, to represent the official state flower, the Red Clover. In the 1890s, the

Vermont (a)   *Vermont (b)*   *Green Mountain Star*

Clover Blossom   *The Mountain Peak*   *Vermont Maple Leaf*

Maple Leaf (a)   *Maple Leaf (b)*   *Maple Leaf (c)*

trend to designate an official flower reflected a growing interest in American's native landscape. Vermont's legislature was the third state to make a choice, honoring a rather commonplace flower, but one that served a variety of uses. The blooms not only decorate the hills with a warm glow; red clover entices bees to make excellent honey and feeds grazing animals. And red clover has provided generations of little girls with blossoms to braid into handmade crowns.

Forests cover three quarters of Vermont's landscape. Vermonters picked the sugar maple for their state tree, honoring another economic and esthetic asset. Vermont maple syrup, made from the tree's sap, has a worldwide reputation, and the tree's fall colors bring tourists every autumn. In 1935, when *Workbasket* magazine planned their All-State Quilt, the editors designed **Vermont Maple Leaf**. The arrangement of four leaves is based on an older **Maple Leaf** (a) design from Clara Stone in 1906. Another arrangement of the same basic leaf pattern is **Maple Leaf** (b) from a 1933 *Kansas City Star*. Nancy Page's **Maple Leaf** (c) is a variation of the Clover Blossom.

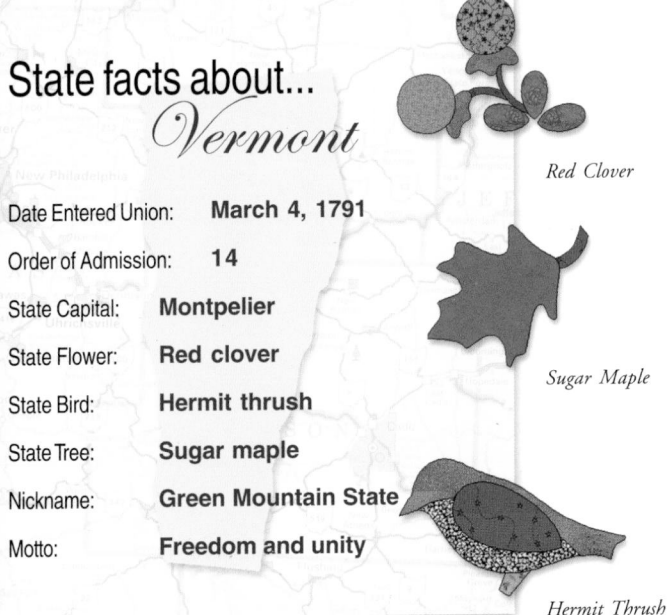

State facts about...
Vermont

Date Entered Union:	**March 4, 1791**
Order of Admission:	**14**
State Capital:	**Montpelier**
State Flower:	**Red clover**
State Bird:	**Hermit thrush**
State Tree:	**Sugar maple**
Nickname:	**Green Mountain State**
Motto:	**Freedom and unity**

Red Clover

Sugar Maple

Hermit Thrush

Richmond Beauty

by Susannah J. Christenson, Lawrence, Kansas, 2001.
Machine-pieced, hand-appliquéd and embroidered, and hand-quilted.
Susannah remembered her Virginia birthplace with Richmond Beauty, bordered with dogwoods and cardinals.
The Richmond Beauty pattern is composed of pieced blocks and appliquéd sashing.

Virginia

Old Dominion

Virginia, "The Old Dominion," has a long and proud history
of quiltmaking, and it's no surprise to find so many patterns
associated with the state.

Jamestown Square

The first English settlement was at
Jamestown, named for the English King in
1607. About 350 years later, Nancy Cabot, the
Chicago Tribune's quilt
columnist, printed **Jamestown
Square**. This pattern recalls the
tiny village that grew into a
prosperous colony with its
capital in Williamsburg. There's
no pattern for Colonial Williamsburg, but you might
include a bit of Williamsburg blue, the dusty blue-
gray color, to remember the Colonial capital.

Richmond

After the Revolutionary War,
Richmond became the state
capital. The city was honored
with a **Richmond** block in
Hearth and Home magazine's
early twentieth-century series
on state capitals. Richmond also served as the
capital of the Confederacy.

Virginia was named for Elizabeth I, England's
virgin queen, by her courtier, Sir Walter Raleigh.
About 1910, a *Hearth and Home* reader sent in a

Virginia block to represent the state. **Virginia Star** was printed in *Country Life* magazine in 1923. A third star, **Star of Virginia**, appeared in *Wallace's Farmer* in 1928.

Virginia

Virginia Star

Star of Virginia

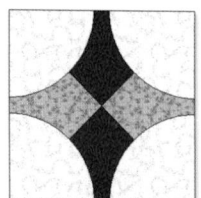
Virginia Snowball

Virginia has several summery floral appliqué blocks named for it, but the only winter block is a pieced **Virginia Snowball** from the *Farmer's Wife* magazine in the 1920s. When several of these blocks are set together in a quilt, a flowing, circular movement appears overall.

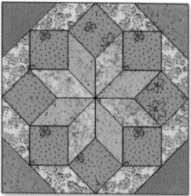
Virginia Reel (b)

Virginia Reel (c)

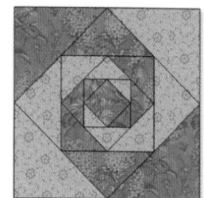
Virginia Reel (d)

Virginia's Choice

Richmond Beauty

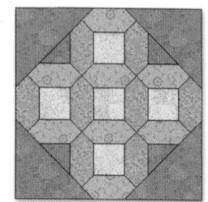
Dogwood (b)

The Virginia Reel is an old dance, and like many dances and fiddle tunes, the name has been given to several quilt patterns, too. The oldest **Virginia Reel** (a) block was in Clara Stone's 1906 booklet,

Practical Needlework: Quilt Patterns. Another **Virginia Reel** (b) is from Mrs. Danner's 1934 catalog. *Workbasket* magazine's 1935 All-State Quilt patterns also had a **Virginia Reel** (c) block.

Virginia Reel (a)

And the Mountain Mist catalog featured another **Virginia Reel** (d).

Choose **Virginia's Choice**, from Nancy Cabot, or **Virginia Worm Fence**, from Clara Stone. A worm fence is a traditional kind of fencing (also called a Virginia fence or a rail fence). It is made of

An old quilt (circa 1890) in a design called "Richmond Beauty" by Mrs. Danner in 1934. The block is all pieced.

"Colonial" interiors like this one, from the 1940s, often featured quilts.

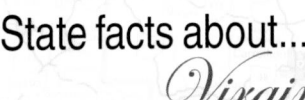

B14:—STATE STREET, BRISTOL, VA.—TENN.

The State line runs down the middle of Bristol with half of Main Street in Virginia; half in Tennessee.

State facts about...
Virginia

Dogwood

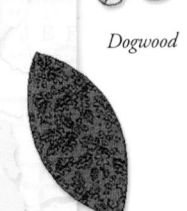

Dogwood

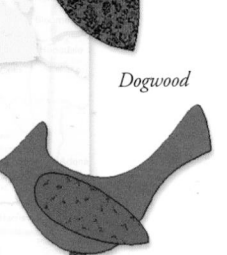

Cardinal

Date Entered Union:	**June 25, 1788**
Order of Admission:	**10**
State Capital:	**Richmond**
State Flower:	**Dogwood**
State Bird:	**Cardinal**
State Tree:	**Dogwood**
Nickname:	**Old Dominion**
Motto:	***Sic semper tyrannis***
	(Thus ever to tyrants)

stacked rails needing no fence posts, and was often built around a log cabin by early settlers. Zigzagging across the hills, Virginia's worm fences look much like the quilt pattern.

Virginia's state tree and state flower are the dogwood. A pieced wreath **Dogwood** (a), from Lockport Batting in the early 1940s, can represent the tree, and another pieced **Dogwood** (b), from the '30s designer Prudence Penny, can represent the flower.

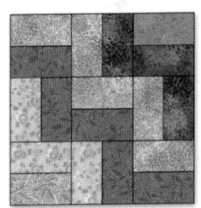

Virginia Worm Fence

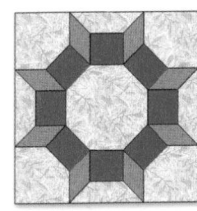

Dogwood (a)

Washington

Evergreen State

Both the state of Washington and the District of Columbia are namesakes of George Washington, who has been honored with several patterns. So if you are looking for Washington designs, you have a number to choose from.

In 1907, *Hearth and Home* magazine asked readers to send patterns named for the states. Abigail Bouthwell Walker Karr responded with **Washington**, which, she noted, was good for a scrap or album quilt.

Washington's Puzzle

Washington's Puzzle, from the Ladies Art Company, and **Washington's Own**, from Carrie Hall's 1935, book *The Romance of the Patchwork Quilt in America*, may have been named for General Washington. This block is also called Coronation and King's Crown, names that may have seemed a bit too royal for

Seattle Skyline with Mt. Rainier in the background.

Washington | Olympia | Spokane

Evergreen | The Mountain Peak | Washington's Own

Columbia

the city that was the state's first American settlement. And although *Hearth and Home* printed **Columbia** to symbolize South Carolina's capital, the pattern can also represent the Columbia River.

Washington Tree

Washington state is known as the Evergreen State. Pieced in shades of green, **Evergreen**, from the Home Art Company in the 1930s, can symbolize the state. **Washington Tree**, from *Woman's Day* magazine in 1942, also represents the nickname. **The Mountain Peak**, from a 1943 *Kansas City Star*, might honor Mt. Ranier, watching over Seattle.

nineteenth-century Americans who preferred to consider that the president who could have been king chose to remain a commoner.

Hearth and Home also asked readers to send blocks named for state capitals. **Olympia** represents the state of Washington. **Spokane**, from the 1930's Nancy Page newspaper column, honors

See also the District of Columbia entry, page 50.

Lake Whatcom, Bellingham, Wash.

Bellingham's rural pleasures about 1915.

Pink Rhododendron

Hemlock

Goldfinch

State facts about...
Washington

Date Entered Union:	**November 11, 1889**
Order of Admission:	**42**
State Capital:	**Olympia**
State Flower:	**Pink rhododendron**
State Bird:	**Willow goldfinch**
State Tree:	**Western hemlock**
Nickname:	**Evergreen State**
Motto:	*Alki* **(By and By)**

West Virginia

West Virginia's green, rolling hills have inspired poets, song writers, and quiltmakers over the years. The state shares a name, and hundreds of years of history, with its neighbor to the east, Virginia.

West Virginia was part of Virginia until 1863. But western Virginians were often unhappy with the far-away eastern government. When secessionist fervor peaked, and the state joined the Southern states to leave the Union at the beginning of the Civil War, 47 northwestern counties seceded from Virginia, declaring themselves a separate state.

The new state was initially to be called Kanawha, after the region's major river. But it was admitted to the Union as West Virginia. You may want to remember the strong Union sentiments that led to West Virginia's secession, with **Union**, first printed in the Ladies Art Company quilt pattern catalog in the late 1880s.

Union

St. Joseph's Hospital, Parkersburg, West Virginia, mailed 1918.

148

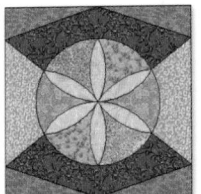

Star of West Virginia

West Virginia Star

Charleston

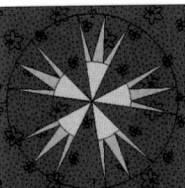

Mountain Pink

Maple Leaf (b)

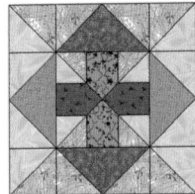

Belle of West Virginia

West Virginia is a pattern sent to *Hearth and Home* about 1910 by Mrs. S.R. of Winfield, West Virginia, who responded to the

West Virginia

magazine's request for reader-submitted state designs. The editors usually chose just one pattern. But someone must have had a warm spot for West Virginia, as the magazine also printed **Belle of West Virginia** and **Star of West Virginia**.

West Virginia Star was recently printed in Carter Houck and Myron Miller's book, *American Quilts and How to Make Them*. They added one to the many, many names found in print for this popular old pattern, also called Virginia Star in Carrie Hall's 1935 book, *The Romance of the Patchwork Quilt in America*. The pattern was also called Stonewall Jackson in the *Chicago Tribune's* Nancy Cabot column in the '30s, perfect for a West Virginia quilt since General Jackson was a native.

The state capital is **Charleston**, honored with a block by *Hearth and Home*. To remember the state's nickname, you might include a **Mountain Pink**, sent

to the Aunt Martha Studios in the early 1930s by a quilter who said the triangles should be pink.

The state bird is the cardinal. You might choose **Arrant Red Birds**, from a 1936 Nancy Cabot column, to suggest this colorful, native bird. Arrant means notoriously bad, a strange characterization

Arrant Red Birds

for a red bird – unless, of course, it's sunrise and you're trying to sleep through some cardinal's songs.

The state tree is the sugar maple. Quilters have many maple leaf designs to choose from. Clara Stone printed **Maple Leaf** (a) in her 1906 booklet *Practical Needlework: Quilt Patterns*. A

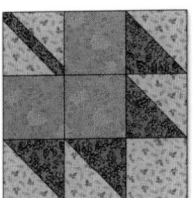

Maple Leaf (a)

few decades later, the Aunt Martha Studios offered a Nine-Patch design called **Maple Leaf** (b).

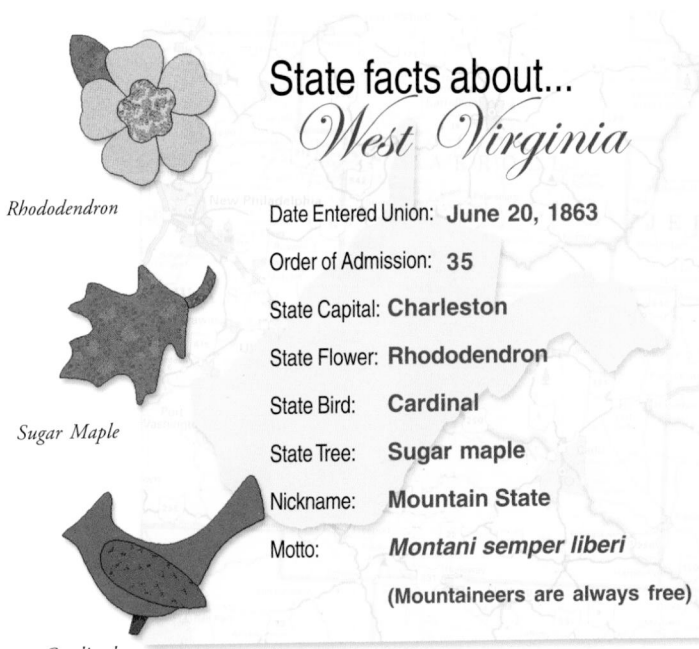

Rhododendron

Sugar Maple

Cardinal

State facts about... *West Virginia*

Date Entered Union: **June 20, 1863**

Order of Admission: **35**

State Capital: **Charleston**

State Flower: **Rhododendron**

State Bird: **Cardinal**

State Tree: **Sugar maple**

Nickname: **Mountain State**

Motto: ***Montani semper liberi***

(Mountaineers are always free)

Wisconsin

The women of Wisconsin have been keeping warm and keeping busy
with quilts during many northern winters.

In the early twentieth century, a reader who called herself Trixie Trix of Oshkosh sent **Wisconsin** in response to *Hearth and Home* magazine's request for state-named patterns. The *Detroit Free Press* printed a block called **Wisconsin Star**.

Madison

Madison, Wisconsin's capital, was honored with an unusual star in *Hearth and Home's* state capital block series. Milwaukee is the state's largest city, so it has its own pattern in **Milwaukee's Own,** from the Ladies Art Company. A **Polka Dots** block, from the Aunt Martha Studios, can represent Milwaukee, famous for its German-American culture, accordions and dancing. Of course, it is also famous for its beer. Rearrange the same patches in the Polka Dots block and you'll make a very popular traditional pattern called **The Drunkard's Path**. We can imagine the nineteenth-century Temperance Movement's opinion of drinking by the name of this block.

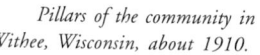

Pillars of the community in Withee, Wisconsin, about 1910.

Wisconsin   Wisconsin Star   Milwaukee's Own

Polka Dots   Drunkard's Path   The Milkmaid's Star

Lady of the Lake (a)   Lady of the Lake (b)   Indian Meadow

Maple Leaf   Ragged Robin   Red Robin

block from Nancy Cabot, or a different **Lady of the Lake** (b) from Ladies Art Company.

The state's name is derived from a Chippewa Indian word meaning "a grassy place." **Indian Meadow**, from a 1931 *Woman's World* magazine, recalls the grassy fields and original settlers whose language left its mark on so many Wisconsin names such as Oshkosh, Wausau and Waukesha.

The state tree is the sugar maple. Clara Stone included a simple but effective **Maple Leaf** pattern in her pamphlet *Practical Needlework: Quilt Patterns*. The state flower is the wood violet. Robert Frank included **Violet Blossoms** in his *E-Z Patterns for Patchwork and Appliqué* (ca. 1935). The state bird

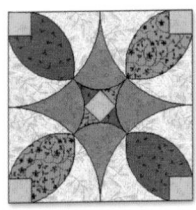

Violet Blossoms

is the robin. The Alice Brooks syndicated column from around the same time included the block **Ragged Robin**. For more literal-minded bird watchers, the syndicated Laura Wheeler column sold a pieced **Red Robin** pattern.

Wisconsin's other famous beverage is milk; the state is home to a huge dairy industry. To represent the dairies, there is **The Milkmaid's Star** from a 1948 *Kansas City Star*. Dairy herds and barns dominate the rural landscape in much of the state. A Barn Raising set for the **Log Cabin** block would make a good tribute to Wisconsin.

Log Cabin blocks set to create Barn Raising variation.

The state's lakes are almost as common as their dairy barns. Wisconsin boasts 8,500 lakes within its borders. Symbolize this magnificent feature of Wisconsin's countryside with a **Lady of the Lake** (a)

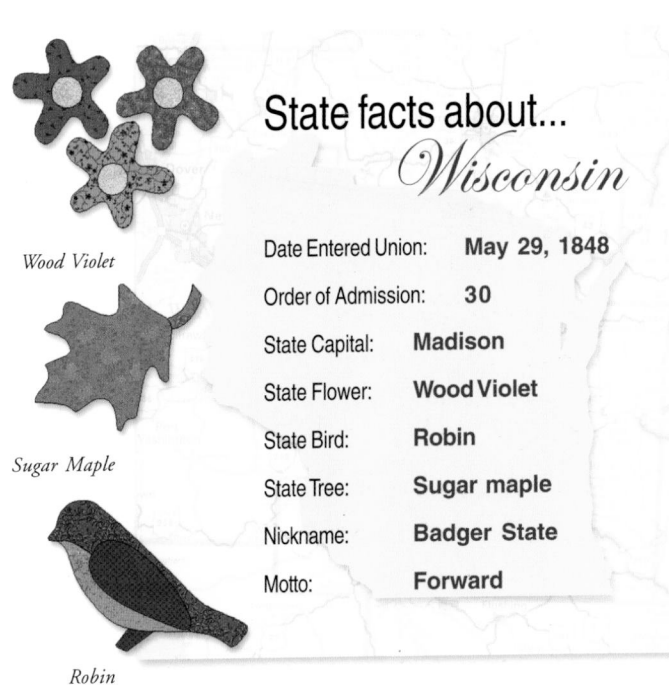

Wood Violet

Sugar Maple

Robin

State facts about...
Wisconsin

Date Entered Union:	**May 29, 1848**
Order of Admission:	**30**
State Capital:	**Madison**
State Flower:	**Wood Violet**
State Bird:	**Robin**
State Tree:	**Sugar maple**
Nickname:	**Badger State**
Motto:	**Forward**

Wyoming

Equality State

The name Wyoming, like so many other American place names,
comes from an Indian word, but not from the language of the Cheyenne,
Arapaho, Sioux, or Shoshone who roamed the area
for centuries before the U.S. settlers.

Wyoming comes from "meacheweam-ing" meaning "big plains" in the language of the Leni-Lanape or Delaware Indians who lived far to the east. The word Wyoming was first used for a valley in Pennsylvania, the original land of the Leni-Lanape. The **Wyoming Valley Block**, named for the area

Wyoming Valley Block

around Wilkes-Barre, Pennsylvania, is from the *Chicago Tribune's* Nancy Cabot column.

Americans migrating in the 1840s and '50s from the eastern United States on the Oregon Trail traveled through what is now Wyoming. They bought provisions at Fort Laramie, wrote their names on Independence Rock, and marveled at the Devil's Gate.

You can remember the summers when a steady stream of wagons jammed the trail with **Oregon Trail** from Carlie Sexton, who wrote about quilt designs in the 1920s and '30s. We know the design better as the Drunkard's Path, but the twists and turns represent well the trail that followed the Platte and Sweetwater Rivers into the Rocky Mountains.

In the late 1860s, the Union Pacific railroad brought permanent settlers to the area. Towns like Cheyenne, Rawlins, and Rock Springs grew up along the tracks. **Railroad Around Rocky Mountain**, sent to *Comfort* magazine in the 1920s, can recall the railroad that brought enough homesteaders for Congress to create the Wyoming Territory in 1868. For more Rocky Mountain designs see the entry for Colorado.

When Wyoming became a territory, women were given the right to vote in territorial elections, a right they did not achieve nationally for 50 more years.

Ladies' Fancy

In 1925, Wyoming was also the first state with a woman governor. Their motto, "Equal Rights," reflects the state's pride in leading this reformation. Surprisingly, there is no recorded quilt pattern referring to women's suffrage, a topic that must have been important to many nineteenth-century quiltmakers. **Ladies' Fancy**, first printed in *Farm and Fireside* magazine in 1884, probably referred only to a woman's right to pick her favorite quilt pattern. But it also can symbolize women's right to choose their elected officials.

In 1890, Wyoming became the 44th state. **Wyoming** was sent to *Hearth and Home* magazine by a reader almost 20 years later. And **Wyoming Patch** was for sale in the Ladies Art Company's pattern catalog about

Oregon Trail — *Wyoming* — *Wyoming Patch*

Cheyenne — *The Sage Bud of Wyoming* — *Buffalo*

Cowboy Star — *Railroad Around Rocky Mountain* — *Indian Paintbrush*

the same time. When set edge to edge, these blocks form a secondary design of stars. **Cheyenne**, the state capital, was honored with a pattern from *Hearth and Home's* series commemorating each state capital.

Workbasket magazine's 1935 All-State Quilt included an old design, **The Sage Bud of Wyoming**, representing the blue-green vegetation that covers the plains. The state flag features a buffalo. You can include a pieced **Buffalo** from designer Prudence Penny's 1933 *Patchwork Zoo* in the *Seattle Post-Intelligencer* newspaper.

The state has several nicknames; one reflected on its license plates is "The Cowboy State." **Cowboy Star** is from the Laura Wheeler newspaper column in the 1930s. The stars appear in the corners when the blocks are set side by side. The state flower, the **Indian Paintbrush**, is represented in another design from Prudence Penny's column.

State facts about...
Wyoming

Date Entered Union:	July 10, 1890
Order of Admission:	44
State Capital:	Cheyenne
State Flower:	Indian paintbrush
State Bird:	Meadowlark
State Tree:	Cottonwood
Nickname:	Equality State
Motto:	Equal rights

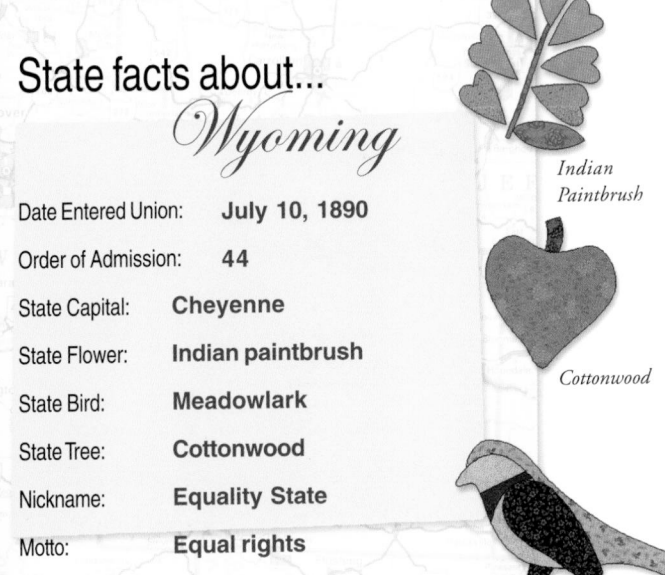

Indian Paintbrush

Cottonwood

Meadowlark

Canada

Canada shares an enduring quilt tradition with the United States. Over the years, U.S. pattern sources have printed many blocks suitable for quilts celebrating Canada.

One of the few blocks literally named for the country is **Canadian Maple Leaf**, published in the little magazine, *Aunt Kate's Quilting Bee*, in 1965 for the Canadian Centennial. The maple leaf is the Canadian national symbol, long a popular image with quilters. Among the oldest **Maple Leaf** patterns are ones from the *Ladies' Home Journal* in 1900 (a), from Clara Stone's 1906 pattern catalog (b), and from the Aunt Martha Company (c) in the 1930s.

Canadian Maple Leaf

If you consider the Canada Goose the unofficial Canadian bird, you can represent it with several old designs. Try **Flying Geese** from the *Oklahoma Farmer Stockman's* "Good Cheer" quilt column in 1929, or **Goose and Goslings** from *Capper's Weekly*.

To give your quilt a historic look, you could use an unusual old pattern that Ruth McKendry found in Durham County, Ontario. She called it **Maple Leaf and Rose** in her 1979 book on Canadian quilts, *Traditional Quilts and Bedcoverings*. Another old block, named **Star of Chamblie**, by Carrie Hall (author of the 1935 index, *The Romance of the Patchwork Quilt in America*) is described by Hall as "an antique design brought to Canada from France in

Maple Leaf and Rose

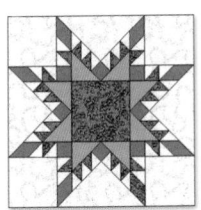

Star of Chamblie

the early part of the nineteenth-century, developed in red, orange, green and white." Her source is obscure, but about the same time, the *Grandmother Clark* catalog called it Etoile de Chamblie.

To represent Canada's three major cultures, piece a **French Star** (a) from Ruby McKim in a 1928 *Kansas City Star*, or a variation (b) pictured in McKendry's book. For the English: **Queen's Crown**, from the Ladies Art Company. And to remember the Native People: **Crossed Canoes** from the Ladies

Queen's Crown

Art Company (also called Indian Canoes in a 1933 *Kansas City Star*). Or use **Hunter's Star** from Carrie Hall (also called Indian Arrowhead by Aunt Martha).

Each province and territory has an official flower, which I've represented in applique. I'm also suggesting a traditional patchwork pattern for each.

Represent Alberta, in the wild west, with a **Cowboy's Star**. One (a) is from *Capper's Weekly*, and the other (b) is from Ruth Finley's 1929 book, *Old Patchwork Quilts*

Rocky Mountain Chain

and the Women Who Made Them. The Rockies snaking through Alberta, British Columbia and the Yukon, can be recalled with **Rocky Mountain Chain** from *Hearth and Home* magazine. Alberta's official

flower is the Wild Rose. You could use **The Rosebud Quilt** from the *Oklahoma Farmer Stockman* in 1932 or **The Rosebud** from the *Kansas City Star* ten years later. Or try **Rosebud** from the Ladies Art Company (a block also called Maple Leaf by Nancy Cabot in 1936).

Maple Leaf (a)   *Maple Leaf (b)*   *Maple Leaf (c)*

Flying Geese   *Goose and Goslings*   *Crossed Canoes*

French Star (a)   *French Star (b)*   *Hunter's Star*

Cowboy's Star (a)   *Cowboy's Star (b)*   *Columbia Puzzle*

For British Columbia (BC), in the far west, use **Columbia Puzzle**, from the Ladies Art Company catalog. BC was settled thanks to the **Pacific Rail Road**, which has a block named for it from Nancy Cabot in 1936. For the beautiful city of Victoria, piece **Queen Victoria** from *Evangeline's* pattern column, a rare 1930s Canadian feature that

Queen Victoria

appeared in the St. John, New Brunswick's, *Maritime Farmer*. To remember the Queen Charlotte Islands, named for the British queen, use **Queen Charlotte's Crown** from Finley. The official BC flower is the Pacific Dogwood. Pieced dogwood blocks include

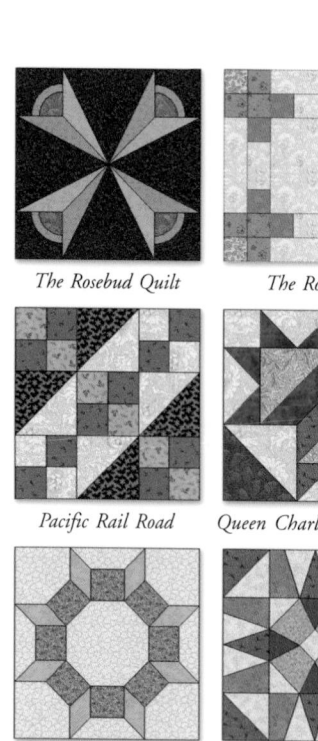

The Rosebud Quilt

The Rosebud

Rosebud

Pacific Rail Road

Queen Charlotte's Crown

Ships A Sailing Quilt

Dogwood (a)

Dogwood (b)

Violet Blossoms

St. John Pavement

Fish Tails

Burr and Thistle

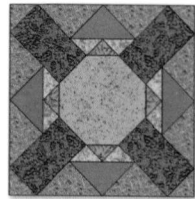

Farmer's Puzzle

Newfoundland, another Atlantic province, was honored with **St. John Pavement**, from the *Maritime Farmer's* "Evangeline's" column.

Nova Scotia's Scottish roots can be pieced in **Burr and Thistle** from the *Rural New Yorker* in 1937. **Star of the East** from *Farm Journal* and **Fish Tails** from a 1933 syndicated Nancy Page column, might represent any of the maritime provinces.

Star of the East

Ontario, north of the Great Lakes, can be seen as the **Lady of the Lake**, with two patterns: one from the Ladies Art Company (a) in 1895, and the second (b) from the *Prairie Farmer* circa 1930.

Lady of the Lake (a)

Prince Edward Island, another fishing capital, is symbolized with **St. Elmo's Fire**, named for the patron saint of sailors.

Quebec has its own design: **Quebec** from the Nancy Cabot column.

Saskatchewan, known as Canada's Bread Basket, can be recalled with **Bread Basket**, the name from Carrie Hall, or **Farm Friendliness**, a pattern from the *Farm Journal*. Saskachewan's official flower, the

Farm Friendliness

Prairie Lily, is well-represented with the classic three-lobed bloom that Ruth Finley named **The Prairie Lily**.

The Northwest Territory's pattern might be **MacKenzie's Square**, which Nancy Cabot named

Dogwood (a) from the Lockport Batting Company and **Dogwood** (b) from the Laura Wheeler/Alice Brooks syndicated pattern column, which also appeared in Canadian newspapers.

For Manitoba, where one of every nine people are involved in agriculture, piece a **Farmer's Puzzle** from Carrie Hall.

New Brunswick, the largest of Canada's three maritime provinces, can be represented by **Ships A Sailing Quilt** from a 1947 *Workbasket* magazine. The province's official flower is the violet, recalled in Robert Frank's **Violet Blossoms** block.

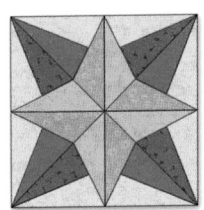

Mariner's Compass

for the explorer who left a mountain range, a bay and a river there as namesakes. **Mariner's Compass**, from Home Art is also called Northern Lights by Nancy Page. The pattern looks very much like the star on the Northwest Territory's coat of arms.

Nunavut is the newest territorial designation for the area close to the Arctic Circle. Remember it with **Pole Star** from *Hearth and Home* magazine, from the 1930s.

The Yukon Territory, in the far North, is symbolized with **North Star** from Lockport Batting Company, or **North Wind** from a 1931 *Kansas City Star*.

Lady of the Lake (b)

St. Elmo's Fire

Quebec

Bread Basket

The Prairie Lily

MacKenzie's Square

Pole Star

North Star

North Wind

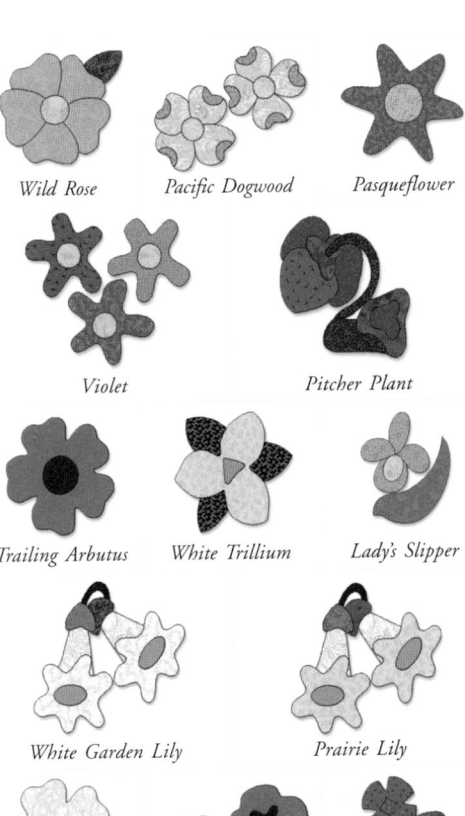

Wild Rose *Pacific Dogwood* *Pasqueflower*

Violet *Pitcher Plant*

Trailing Arbutus *White Trillium* *Lady's Slipper*

White Garden Lily *Prairie Lily*

Mountain Avens *Arctic Poppy* *Fireweed*

Maple

Goose

Facts about...
Canada

Provinces:	Established:	Flower:
Alberta	1905	**Wild rose**
British Columbia	1871	**Pacific dogwood**
Manitoba	1870	**Pasqueflower**
New Brunswick	1867	**Violet**
Newfoundland	1949	**Pitcher plant**
Nova Scotia	1867	**Trailing arbutus**
Ontario	1867	**White trillium**
Prince Edward Island	1873	**Lady's slipper**
Quebec	1867	**White garden lily**
Saskatchewan	1905	**Prairie lily**

Territories:		
Northwest Territories	1869	**Mountain avens**
Nunavut	1999	**Arctic poppy**
Yukon	1898	**Fireweed**

157

Rolling Stone

by Barbara Brackman, Lawrence, Kansas, 2001.
Machine-pieced and appliquéd by Barbara, machine-quilted by Pamela Mayfield.
Made for a geologist who's lived in eleven states, the Rolling Stone is bordered
with the leaves and pine cones from oaks, cottonwoods, palmettos and evergreens.

Wanderers

Many of us bloom where we are planted. But America is a nation
on the road. And since the average American moves once every five years, your
family quilt may well use blocks and symbols from several home states,
celebrating the fact that you have moved so often.

My own addresses include New York, Ohio, Kansas, California, Illinois, Wisconsin and Washington. Shauna Christensen's family has lived in Utah, Washington, California and Kansas. So her quilt, *Home is where ... ♥*, includes symbols for all four states mixed

*Home is where ...♥,
by Shauna O.
Christensen, 2000,
Lawrence, KS.*

in the border. Rather than choosing a block from any particular state for the center, she pieced a Log Cabin, the classic symbol of hearth and home.

You could also use any pictorial house block to symbolize home. Try **Old Home** from *Comfort* magazine, or Ruby McKim's **House on the Hill**. Or, you might prefer a more abstract representation, such as **Home Again** from *Farm Journal*, **Home Maker** from Clara

Old Home

Stone, **Home Treasure**, a Nancy Cabot revision of an old Ladies Art Company block, or **Star of the Home** from the Ladies Art Company.

159

Houses

by Barbara Brackman, Lawrence, Kansas, 1976.
I embroidered 25 addresses in five states on the house doors of this quilt.
Since then I've added five more addresses and two more states.

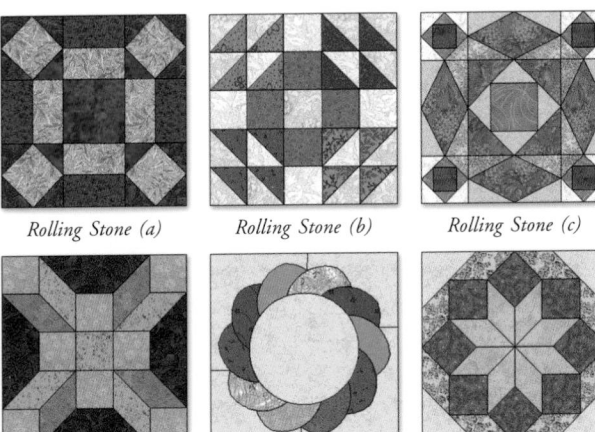

Rolling Stone (a) Rolling Stone (b) Rolling Stone (c)

Rolling Stone (d) Rolling Stone (e) Rolling Stone (f)

Wandering Foot. Its malign influence was believed to invoke a tendency toward a discontented, unstable and roving disposition. The way to take the curse off the design was to call it Turkey Tracks."

Other designs celebrating the freedom to explore are **The Wanderer**, a set for fans from *Comfort* magazine, and **Wanderer's Path in the Wilderness**, an old name for what we often call the Drunkard's Path, published first by *Farm and Home* magazine in 1888. **Wandering Flower** is from the *Kansas City Star* in 1939.

Wandering Flower

Nancy Cabot` symbolizes the nomad tradition with **Pathfinder**. Piece Ruby McKim's **Rambler** or the *Kansas City Star's* **Rambling Road**.

Star of the Home

There are blocks, such as Rolling Stone, that symbolize moving and wandering. I made a quilt for a friend who has lived in eleven states working as a geologist, for example, by choosing the Rolling Stone block for the quilt's center. I let the border represent trees from the states he'd lived in. **Rolling Stone**, perfect for any traveler, comes in several versions which appeared in the Ladies Art Company catalog (a), the *Farmer's Wife* (b), Ruth Finley's book (c) (a version also called Storm at Sea), Joseph Doyle catalog (d), the *Kansas City Star* (e) in 1939, and a pattern catalog from "Grandma Dexter" (f).

Wandering Foot

If you are always on the lookout for greener grass, consider appliquéing the classic **Wandering Foot** block. Quilt historian Ruth Finley wrote of a "quaint superstition" about the pattern. "No child of tender years was permitted to sleep under a

House on the Hill Home Again Home Maker

Home Treasure The Wanderer Pathfinder

Rambler Wanderer's Path in the Wilderness Rambling Road

161

Block Index

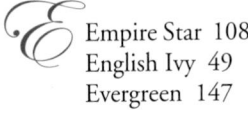

Symbol Index

References

Barbara Bannister and Edna Paris Ford, *The United States Patchwork Pattern Book*, New York: Dover Publications, 1976. Fifty patterns from *Hearth and Home*.

Barbara Bannister and Edna Paris Ford, *State Capitals Quilt Blocks*, New York: Dover Publications, 1977. Fifty more patterns from *Hearth and Home*.

Workbasket Magazine, *U.S. State Quilt Blocks*, Kansas City: KC Publishing, 1988. Patterns from the All-State Quilt.

Installing the Magic Book™ software

1. Insert the disc into your computer's CD-ROM drive.
2. Click on Start.
3. Point to Settings.
4. Click on Control Panel.
5. Double-click the Add/Remove Programs icon.
6. Click on the Install button.
7. Follow the instructions on the screen.

Enjoy another Magic Book!

Stitched with Love: A Mother's Quilting Legacy
Designs by Robyn Pandolph

Folk art appliqué from one of America's top-selling designers. Read the book, then enter Robyn's world on the CD. Quilts, wallhangings, craft projects, design ideas for mothers, grandmothers and children. This easy-to-use Magic Book software on a CD-ROM includes complete patterns ready for printing in any size you choose, Robyn's step-by-step video demonstrating needle turn appliqué, coloring tools to let you recolor Robyn's designs, and much more!

More Software from The Electric Quilt Company

ELECTRIC QUILT
Complete quilt design program
Includes over 10,000 quilt blocks and fabrics that are ready for you to design with, so it's easy for the beginner. If you need more advanced tools, you can draw your own design, scan your own fabric, design your own quilt layout. Foundation piecing, appliqué, yardage calculation – EQ does it all!

BLOCKBASE
The world's largest pieced patterns collection
Barbara Brackman's *Encyclopedia of Pieced Quilt Patterns* on CD. All new Windows version. Over 4,000 quilt patterns – ready to print. Rotary cutting instructions. Foundation patterns. Templates. Hundreds of search options.

To Order a Full Catalog or Place an Order

The Electric Quilt Company
419 Gould Street, Suite 2
Bowling Green, OH 43402 USA
sales@electricquilt.com

Phone: 419-352-1134
(M-F 9am to 5pm EST)
Fax: 419-352-4332
To order: 800-356-4219

www.electricquilt.com

Our products are available at a quilt store near you.